Worcester

CITY ON THE RISE

ALLEN FLETCHER

ALLEN FLETCHER

ISBN # 0-9668420-3-0
Library of Congress Control Number: 2005932798

Worcester — City on the Rise
A publication of
Worcester Publishing Ltd.
172 Shrewsbury St.
Worcester, Ma. 01604
Publishers of *Worcester Magazine* and the *Worcester Business Journal.*
Publisher: Mark Murray
Editor: Allen Fletcher
Art Director: Chris Miller
Profiles Editor and Copy Editor: Lester Paquin
Profiles Author: Jennifer Lucarelli Shimer
Profiles Designer: Sean Harvey
Account Representatives: Mark Murray, Bonnie Leroux, Sally Tyler and Christine Gentuso

Printed in the U.S.A by Walsworth Publishing Company, Marceline, MO.
Dustjacket printed by LaVigne Press, Worcester, MA.

ALLEN FLETCHER

ALLEN FLETCHER

Worcester — City on the rise.

n 1955, *National Geographic* magazine celebrated the proud industrial heritage of the Heart of the Commonwealth with an article titled, "Cities like Worcester make America." Fifty years later, it is time to celebrate this same city's re-birth, as a former center of manufacturing re-invents itself as a center of health care, bio-technology and more.

From its agrarian roots and an entrepreneurial tradition founded at the headwaters of the Blackstone River, Worcester grew steadily into an industrial engine whose enterprise and output rivaled that of any similar-sized city in the country. From barbed wire to the monkey wrench, its inventions and products equipped the nation; and its busy mills drew a steady and diverse stream of immigrants seeking to put down roots in the New World.

This creative energy and this diverse population conspired to forge an industrious and decidedly blue-collar city whose heyday extended through the post-World War II prosperity of the 1950s. It wasn't long thereafter that it began to experience the same flight of manufacturing and loss of retail vitality that befell most cities in the Northeast. Its population eroded. It began to explore the nascent field of biotechnology to replace its declining industry. It grasped at notions such as a downtown mall as keys to rejuvenation.

PROMOTIONAL PUBLICATION OF THE WORCESTER BOARD OF TRADE – 1909.

ere at the beginning of a new century, the city finds itself riding a wave of optimism. Fresh political leadership and a rising tide of economic development investment have contributed to a palpable sense that the city has recovered its equilibrium and is moving forward with a renewed sense of confidence. Its economy is transmuting and reviving. Its decrepit train station has been magnificently renovated; its moribund mall is being dismantled and replaced; and its vacant mill buildings are being converted to a rich mixture of new uses.

The Worcester of the 21st century is characterized by old bones and new blood. The city's commercial heart boasts an energetic mixture of architectural styles, wearing the patina and provenance of a rich history — some of it storied, some almost forgotten. Mechanics Hall, which went from presenting Charles Dickens in the 19th century to professional wrestling in the 20th, has been restored to stature as a signature concert hall and the preferred recording venue for the likes of Itzhak Perlman. Downtown's Commerce Building sits on the site of Brinley Hall, which hosted the country's first women's rights convention. The historic courthouse on Main Street saw the first judicial repudiation of slavery in the nation; Isaiah Thomas gave the first New England reading of the Declaration of Independence on the site of the current City Hall; and, of course, George Washington rested his weary bones here while transporting cannon through town during the Revolutionary War.

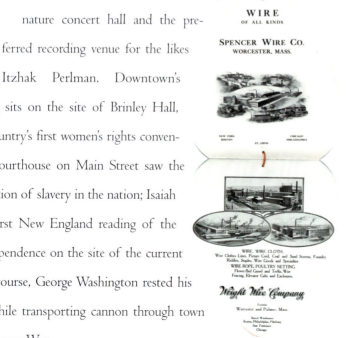

THE CITYSQUARE PROJECT SEEKS TO RE-ESTABLISH A RETAIL STREET GRID BETWEEN THE COMMON AND WASHINGTON SQUARE.

lm Park, the first urban land purchased for park purposes in the country and improved by the firm of Frederick Law Olmstead, sits near the site of the ball field where Jonathan Lee Richmond pitched the first perfect game in major league base-ball history. Within a few short blocks of the canal district, one can pass the building where the anar-chist Emma Goldman ran her ice cream shop and plotted the assassination of the head of Standard Oil; the lot where Poet Laureate Stanley Kunitz watched the approach of Halley's Comet as a young boy; and the building where the Rolling Stones played their unannounced local gig in 1981.

To its great pride, Worcester also remains a city of strong neighborhoods. Its famous seven hills are lined with three-deckers — the utilitarian housing style emblematic of its blue-collar past — and its tonier West Side is graced by a variety of hous-ing styles on its quieter, tree-lined streets. Those in the know can point out where rocket pioneer Robert Goddard used to take his daily walk, where world cycling champion Major Taylor lived, and where activists set off a bomb under the porch of Sacco-Vanzetti judge Webster Thayer.

At the dawn of the 20th century, Worcester boasted the largest percentage of foreign-stock residents of any city in the United States — being led in numbers by Italians, Irish and French-Canadians — with each group bringing with it its cus-toms, its religion and its passion to succeed in a new life. At the beginning of the 21st century, those populations have been largely assimilated into the city's mainstream, with their newcomers' torch being passed to Hispanics, Southeast Asians, Africans, Albanians and Brazilians. Storefronts where Jewish merchants once presided now feature Vietnamese and Ghanaian goods. The first Armenian church in the country now accommodates an Islamic mosque.

THE BLACKSTONE CANAL PROJECT WOULD RE-CREATE THE HISTORIC CANAL SOUTH OF UNION STATION.

emographic and economic patterns have shifted. Whereas the city's largest employers long came from the ranks of heavy industry, they now represent the medical and insurance fields, and the birth control pill has long since replaced barbed wire as the emblem of entrepreneurial invention. A population once concentrated near inner-city industry has now dispersed and suburbanized; and the city has relaxed its gravitational pull on its surrounding towns. Whereas regional shopping malls have eroded Worcester's strength as a retail magnet, it has enjoyed a resurgence of prominence as an entertainment center for the region. The DCU Center remains a regional draw as a concert/event venue; the downtown club district keeps the area alive long into the night; Shrewsbury Street boasts a thriving restaurant scene; and the Canal District is blossoming with possibilities.

A CABLE-STAYED SKYBRIDGE WOULD CONNECT THE NEW HILTON GARDENS INN WITH THE CONVENTION CENTER.

The growth of upscale offerings is emblematic of the advent of yet another immigrant — the young urban professional — enticed by the success of commuter rail service to the east, attractive housing values, the rural charms of the surrounding county, the city's fundamental livability and its cultural and recreational resources. Its art scene is thriving, anchored by a first-class art museum and the oldest crafts school in the country. Its legacy of parks and woodlands offers convenient access to the pleasures of nature, whether it takes the form of canoeing down into the Blackstone Valley, boating on Lake Quinsigamond, skiing on Mount Wachusett or hiking and mountain-biking in the wilds of Cascades Park. The city's wealth of colleges and universities remains an extraordinary cultural resource as well as a fount of rejuvenation for its population. The proud tradition of local amateur sports is stronger than ever; and professional baseball — for decades a frustrated civic dream — has finally made a triumphant return to the city in the form of the Worcester Tornadoes, 2005 champions of the CanAm League.

n the midst of a tentative, gathering glamour, the city retains the gritty essence that has long endeared it to those with a taste for unpretentious charms: Its diners, its corner pubs, its fish-and-chips joints are familiar comforts to those in the know — acquired tastes for visitors who take the time to discover them. One can still find most anything here among its unheralded treasure trove of supply stores and mechanics' shops. Its back alleys and urban artifacts remain a playground for those with a nose for urban archeology and fallow fields for the renaissance which seems to be in the air.

A new optimism is everywhere. With this book, we at Worcester Publishing celebrate this pivotal moment in the history of the Heart of the Commonwealth — the moment when a great city re-establishes its bearings and invents itself once again. ●

CHRISTINA O'NEILL

LIKE ROME,
WORCESTER WAS BUILT
ON SEVEN HILLS:
PAKACHOAG,
SAGATABSCOT,
HANCOCK, CHANDLER,
GREEN, BANCROFT
AND NEWTON.

LORA BRUECK

SUCCESSIVE ERAS OF DEVELOPMENT HAVE PRODUCED AN ECLECTIC AND JUMBLED CITYSCAPE.

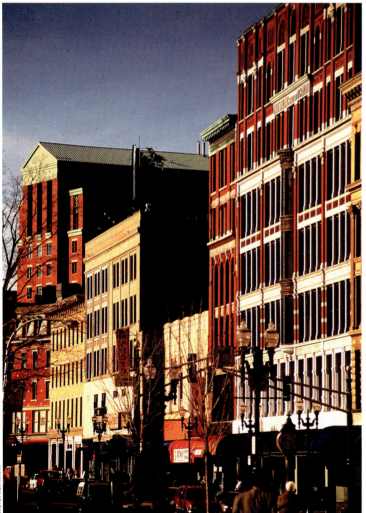

OLD AND NEW
BUILDINGS ARE
JUXTAPOSED
DOWNTOWN IN A
RICH COLLAGE.

CLASSICAL DETAILS ENLIVEN THE DOWNTOWN ARCHITECTURAL MIX.

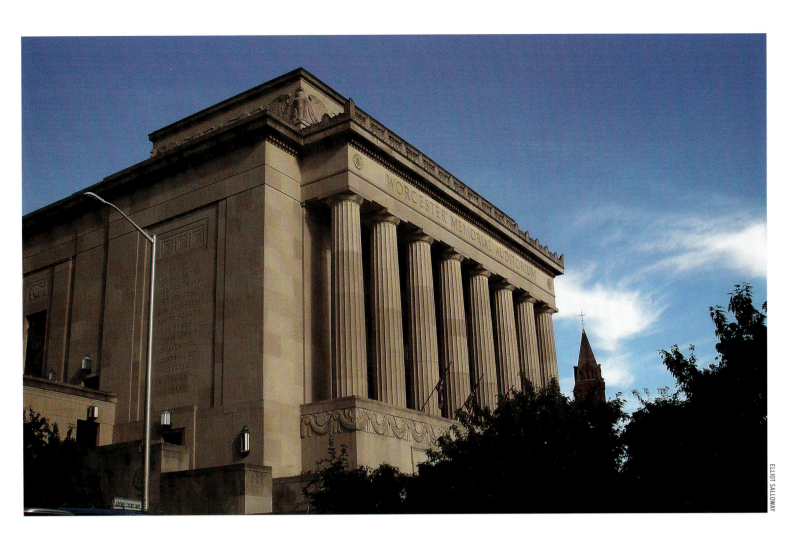

ALLEN FLEETCHER

RICK ENGLISH

MIKE MULCAHY

ELLIOT SALLOWAY

GERALD GROCCIA

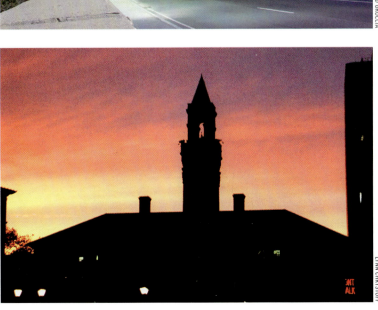

LYNN CHRYSTOFF

ELLIOT SALLOWAY

TAMMY WOODARD

ERIKA SIDOR

ERIKA SIDOR

CLARK
UNIVERSITY
1887

ERIKA SIDOR

DORIS O'KEEFE

ERIKA SIDOR

ERIKA SIDOR

THE CITY'S NECKLACE OF PARKS OFFERS RESPITE IN ALL SEASONS; ITS CHURCHES REPRESENT VARIED RELIGIONS.

BILL MIXON

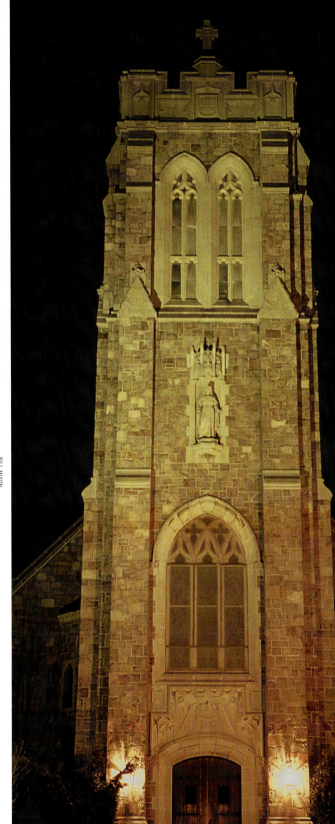

MARI SEDER

BILL MIXON

DONNA DIRADO

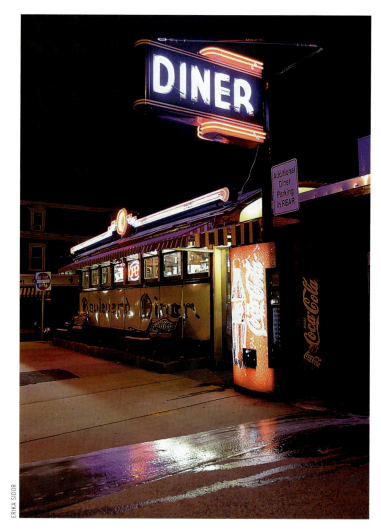

ERIKA SIDOR

JEFF LOUGHLIN

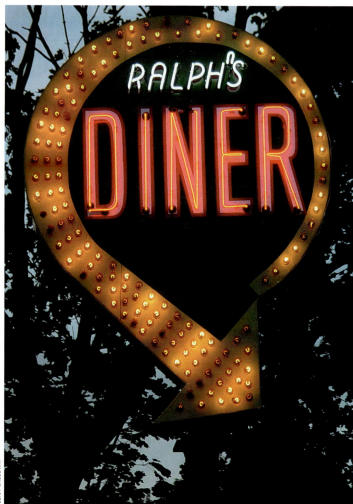

ELLIOT SALLOWAY

ELLIOT SALLOWAY

JEFF LOUGHLIN

ALLEN FLETCHER

CHRISTOPHER NAVIN

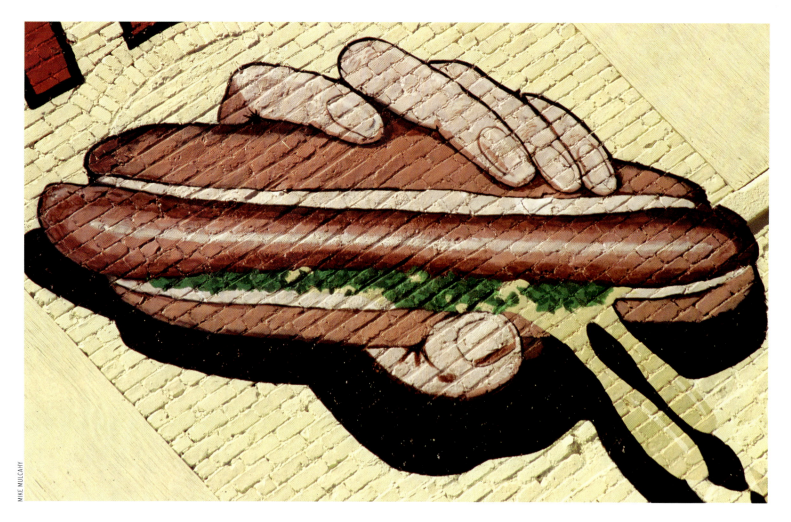

MIKE MULCAHY

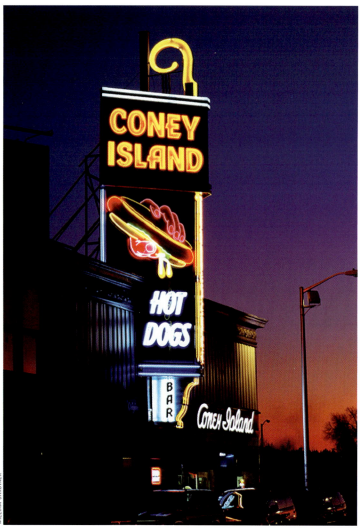

WILLIAM GARDINER

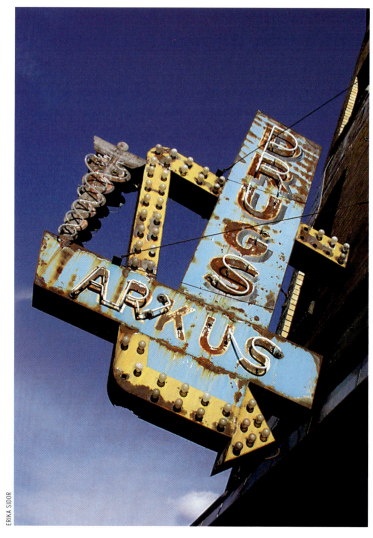

ERIKA SIDOR

HOT DOGS,
KIELBASA AND
HOME FRIES LAY A
SOLID FOUNDATION
OF BLUE COLLAR
CUISINE.

TAMMY WOODARD

TAMMY WOODARD

JEFF LOUGHLIN

Upscale establishments contribute to a dining scene that is rapidly expanding beyond diner fare. The gritty bones of the city (following pages) provide a foothold in the past and an opportunity for renaissance.

ALLEN FLETCHER

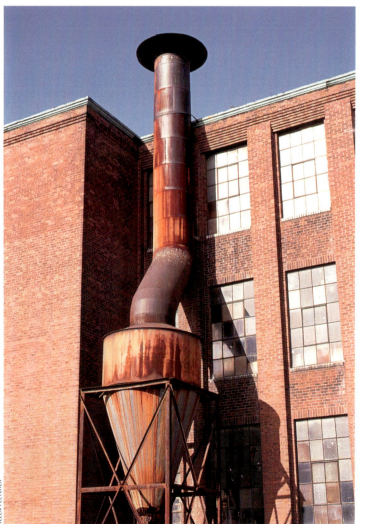

ALLEN FLETCHER

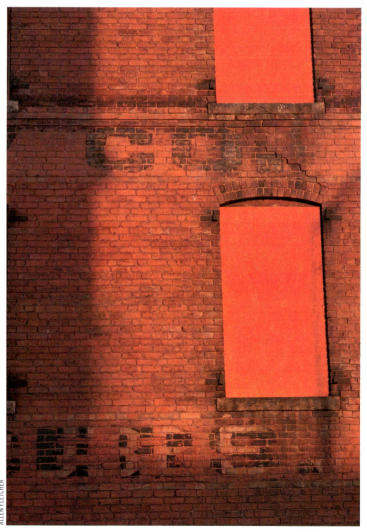

ALLEN FLETCHER

ALLEN FLETCHER

ALLEN FLETCHER

ALLEN FLETCHER

CHRISTINA O'NEILL

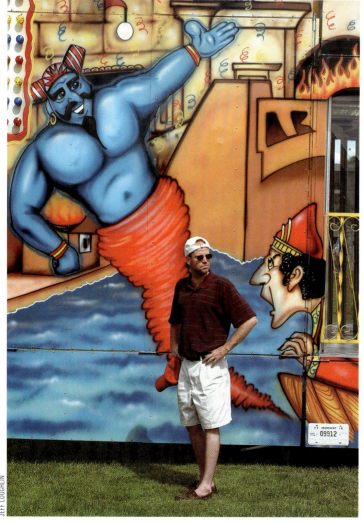

JEFF LOUGHLIN

ALLEN FLETCHER

ERIKA SIDOR

TAMMY WOODARD

TAMMY WOODARD

CHRISTOPHER NAVIN

TROY THOMPSON

CHRISTOPHER NAVIN

JEFF LOUGHLIN

JEFF LOUGHLIN

JEFF LOUGHLIN

WORCESTER IS FAMOUS FOR ITS THREE-DECKERS — THE UTILITARIAN
HOUSING STYLE ONCE REVILED AS A BLIGHT AND NOW BEING ADAPTED TO
CONDO-OWNERSHIP. FOLLOWING PAGES: A VARIETY OF HISTORICAL
HOUSING TYPES POPULATE THE CITY'S LANDSCAPE.

ERIKA SIDOR

ERIKA SIDOR

ALLEN FLETCHER

ALLEN FLETCHER

ALLEN FLETCHER

MARI SEDER

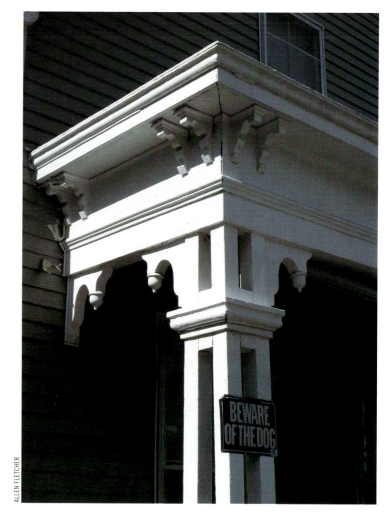

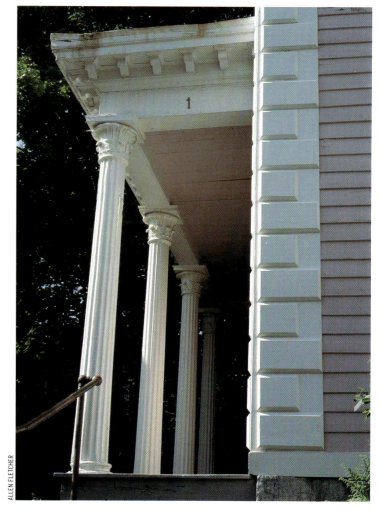

SCOTT ERB

MIKE MULCAHY

MIKE MULCAHY

MIKE MULCAHY

LARRY KNIVETON

DORIS O'KEEFE

THE SURROUNDING TOWNS OFFER

A WIDE VARIETY OF RURAL ANTIDOTES

TO URBAN LIFE:

FACING PAGE, TOP TO BOTTOM: FRUITLANDS MUSEUM

IN HARVARD; THE OLD STONE CHURCH

IN WEST BOYLSTON; THE WILLARD CLOCK MUSEUM

IN GRAFTON.

THIS PAGE, CLOCKWISE FROM TOP: ST. JOSEPH'S

ABBEY IN SPENCER; TOWER HILL BOTANIC GARDEN

IN BOYLSTON; AND A WINTER SCENE IN SUTTON.

MARTY THORNTON

DANIELA MUNOZ MAINES

JEFF LOUGHLIN

FACING PAGE, CLOCKWISE FROM TOP:
TOWER HILL IN BOYLSTON; OLD
STURBRIDGE VILLAGE IN STURBRIDGE;
AND MOUNT WACHUSETT IN PRINCETON.
THIS PAGE, CLOCKWISE FROM TOP:
INTER-SPECIES CONTACT AT THE
ECOTARIUM; MEDIEVAL FUN AT THE
HIGGINS ARMORY MUSEUM; AND THE
SPRING PLANT SALE AT TOWER HILL.

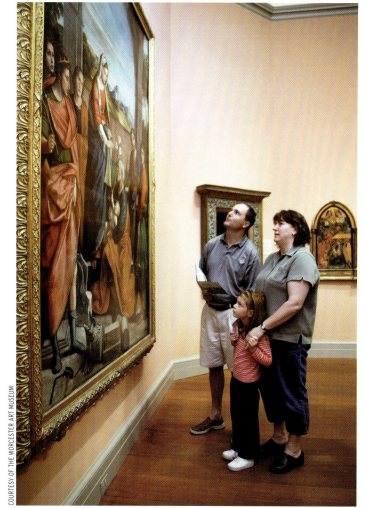

FACING PAGE: THE WORCESTER ART MUSEUM FEATURES A BROAD SPECTRUM OF ART FOR VISITORS. THIS PAGE: THE WORCESTER CENTER FOR CRAFTS OFFERS BOTH EXPERT INSTRUCTION AND CRAFT ITEMS FOR SALE.

CHRISTINA O'NEILL

CHRISTINA O'NEILL

ERIKA SIDOR

ERIKA SIDOR

GOOD WEATHER BRINGS OUT THE CROWDS.
FACING PAGE: stART ON THE STREET ARTS FAIR.
THIS PAGE: JAZZ AT SUNSET AT THE ECOTARIUM AND
SHREWSBURY STREET'S COLUMBUS DAY PARADE.

THIS PAGE: THE ANNUAL FIRST NIGHT CELEBRATION BRINGS THE DOWNTOWN ALIVE, INDOORS AND OUT. FACING PAGE, CLOCKWISE FROM TOP: FREDERICK HAYES DANCE COMPANY AT THE AFRICAN-AMERICAN FESTIVAL; INDIAN DANCE AT THE WORCESTER ART MUSEUM; NIPMUC GATHERING IN GRAFTON.

ALLEN FLETCHER

ALLEN FLETCHER

ALLEN FLETCHER

THIS PAGE: ANNUAL LATINO-AMERICAN
FESTIVAL TRANSFORMS MAIN STREET.
FACING PAGE: SUMMER NATIONALS
AUTO SHOW TAKES OVER GREEN HILL
PARK ON THE FOURTH OF JULY.

JEFF LOUGHLIN

ALLEN FLETCHER

ALLEN FLETCHER

ALLEN FLETCHER

ALLEN FLETCHER

THE MASSACHUSETTS SYMPHONY
ORCHESTRA HOLDS FORTH (CLOCKWISE
FROM TOP) IN MECHANICS HALL,
INSTITUTE PARK AND CRISTOFORO
COLUMBO PARK.

DOWNTOWN'S DCU CENTER
BRINGS A WIDE VARIETY OF
NATIONAL ACTS TO THE
WORCESTER STAGE.

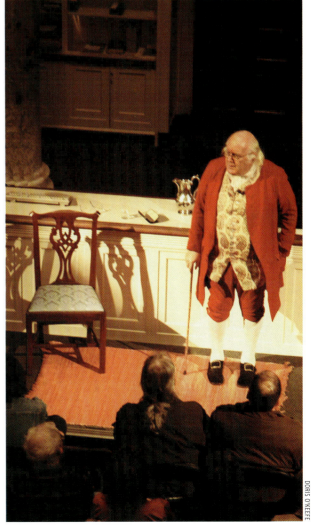

LOCAL THEATRICAL ACTIVITY IN
A VARIETY OF VENUES.
FACING PAGE: *THE TEMPEST*, AT GREEN
HILL PARK; AND *CABARET*, AT
FOOTHILLS THEATRE COMPANY.
THIS PAGE: *RAGTIME*, AT FOOTHILLS;
TWELFTH NIGHT AT CLARK UNIVERSITY;
AND BEN FRANKLIN AT THE AMERICAN
ANTIQUARIAN SOCIETY.

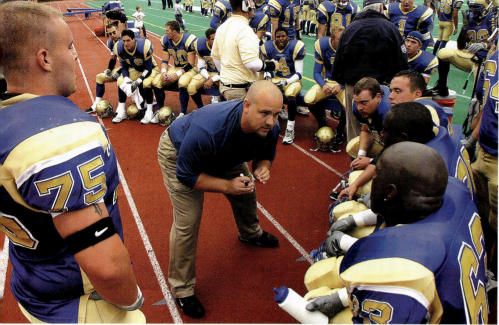

ERIKA SIDOR

CHRISTOPHER NAVIN

ERIKA SIDOR

MICHAEL SEFTON

MICHAEL SEFTON

THE LOCAL SPORTS SCENE IS RICH IN TRADITION AND LORE, WHILE THE WORCESTER TORNADOES (FACING PAGE) ARE 2005 CHAMPIONS OF THE NEWLY-FORMED CANAM LEAGUE.

ALLEN FLETCHER

ALLEN FLETCHER

ALLEN FLETCHER

MICHAEL SEFTON

ALLEN FLETCHER

DANIELA MUNOZ MAINES

COURTESY OF THE ECOTARIUM

COURTESY OF BLACKSTONE HERITAGE CORRIDOR

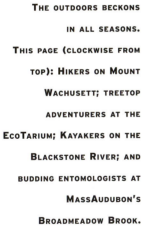

THE OUTDOORS BECKONS IN ALL SEASONS. THIS PAGE (CLOCKWISE FROM TOP): HIKERS ON MOUNT WACHUSETT; TREETOP ADVENTURERS AT THE ECOTARIUM; KAYAKERS ON THE BLACKSTONE RIVER; AND BUDDING ENTOMOLOGISTS AT MASSAUDUBON'S BROADMEADOW BROOK.

DOUG KIMBALL

DAN VAILLANCOURT

KIRA BEUADOIN

WILLIAM GARDINER

This page, clockwise from top: Heavy metal at the Lucky Dog Music Hall; Big band jazz at Union Blues; and local legend Emil Haddad performs at the EcoTarium's Jazz at Sunset. Facing page, clockwise from top: Respite at Ralph's; a pas de deux at Club Marque; and a Chinese acrobat at Mechanics Hall.

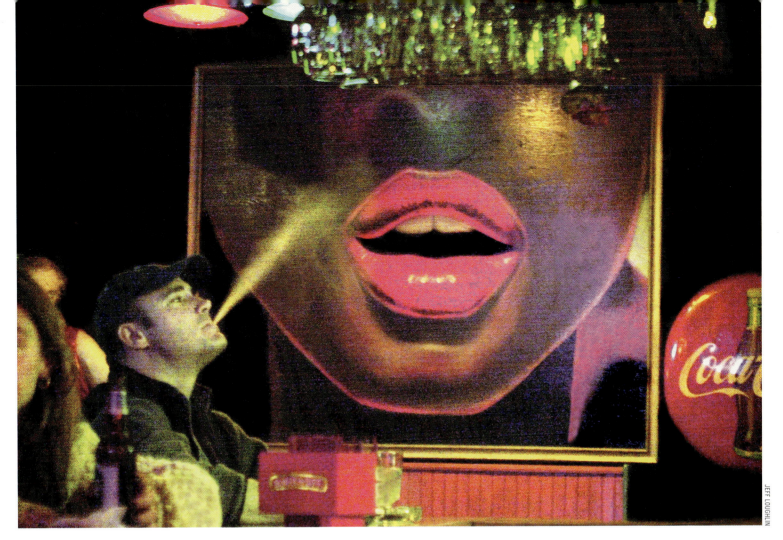

JEFF LOUGHLIN

JEFF LOUGHLIN

JEFF LOUGHLIN

JEFF LOUGHLIN

JEFF LOUGHLIN

JEFF LOUGHLIN

ERIKA SIDOR

TIM MULCAHY

ALLEN FLETCHER

JEFF LOUGHLIN

JEFF LOUGHLIN

JEFF LOUGHLIN

JEFF LOUGHLIN

MICHAEL SEFTON

JEFF LOUGHLIN

ALLEN FLETCHER

ERIKA SIDOR

CLOCKWISE FROM TOP LEFT:
FULL HOUSE AT THE BOULEVARD
DINER; CHEF JOHN PICCOLO;
BARTENDER THIDA SOU AT VINCENT'S;
GRILLMAN STEVE TURNER AT
CHARLIE'S DINER; AND OWNERS MATT
DIVRIS AND JEFF MARARIAN OF THE
BLACKSTONE TAP.

**CLOCKWISE FROM TOP LEFT:
OWNER ED HYDER AT HIS
MEDITERRANEAN MARKET; GEORGE
SIGEL OF FAIRWAY BEEF; JOE DUCAS
OF WIDOFF'S BAKERY; TOM HADDAD OF
TOM'S INTERNATIONAL DELI; AND
ERICK GODIN OF THE LUCKY DOG
MUSIC HALL.**

MAYOR TIM MURRAY

BANKER/ENTREPRENEUR DAVID "DUDDIE" MASSAD

DPW CHIEF BOB MOYLAN

ATTORNEY BOB LONGDEN WITH CITYSQUARE DEVELOPER YOUNG PARK

LOCAL TORNADO ALEX DE LOS SANTOS

ARTS ADVOCATES DAVID LEATCH, ERIN WILLIAMS AND ANGIE BILOTTA

The African Cultural Center's Emil Igwenagu

WICN host and singer Monica hatch

Local news favorite Ben Dobson

City Clerk David Rushford

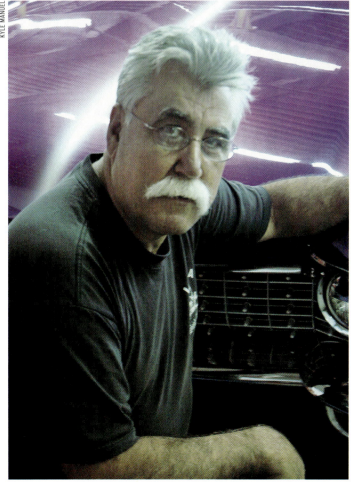

Motorhead Bob Moscoffian

STATE SENATOR HARRIETTE CHANDLER WITH TORNADOES OWNER ALAN STONE

CITY MANAGER MIKE O'BRIEN

ST. PATRICK'S DAY GRAND MARSHAL TIM COONEY

DISTRICT ATTORNEY JOHN CONTE

CHANNEL 3 REPORTER JULIE TREMMEL

LOCUTOR DE RADIO ANDRÉS PEREZ

RESTAURATEUR DAVE LEMENAGER

DCU CENTER MANAGER SANDY DUNN

THE WORCESTER ART MUSEUM'S JIM WELU

SUPERMARKET OWNER EDIBERTO SANTIAGO

WPI JAZZ HOUND RICH FALCO

DISTRICT 4 CITY COUNCILOR BARBARA HALLER

CHEF VENICE FOUCHARD

ROCK IMPRESARIO DAN HARTWELL

CLUB OWNER VINCENT HEMMETER

LATINO CULTURAL DUEÑA DOLLY VAZQUEZ

ARTS PROMOTOR GARY DUSOE

WORCESTER MAGAZINE EDITOR MICHAEL WARSHAW WITH *T&G* COLUMNIST
DIANNE WILLIAMSON

TORNADOES MANAGER RICH GEDMAN

CITY COUNCILOR-AT-LARGE KONSTANTINA LUKES

SCHOOL COMMITTEEWOMAN OGRETTA MCNEIL

BOXING CHAMP JOSE RIVERA

NEW SHERIFF GUY GLODIS

MAIN SOUTH ACTIVIST BILLY BREAULT

BIOTECH ADVOCATE KEVIN O'SULLIVAN

SPORTS COLUMNIST AND MASS. BOXING COMMISSIONER NICK MANZELLO

TOURISM PROMOTOR JEANNIE HEBERT

BLUES MAN AL ARSENAULT

ATTORNEY HECTOR PINEIRO

SCHOOL ADMINISTRATOR STACIE LUSTER

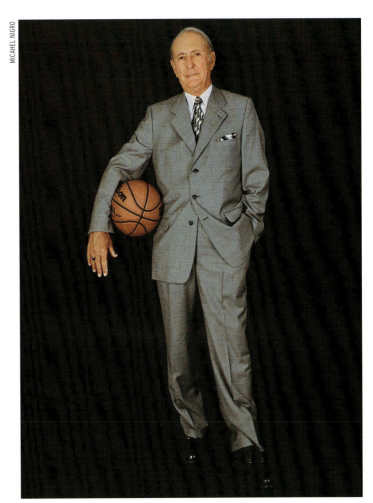

MR. BASKETBALL BOB COUSY

RADIO HOST AND FORMER POLICE CHIEF ED GARDELLA

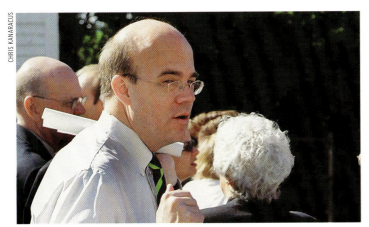

U.S. CONGRESSMAN JIM MCGOVERN

JAZZ PIANIST LOU TERRICCIANO

GLENN PERRY

DAN VAILLANCOURT

LARRY KNIVETON

LARRY KNIVETON

AND THROUGH IT ALL, THE REGION IS

WRAPPED IN THE BLESSINGS OF THE SEASONS:

SUMMER — THE TIME OF SUN-BAKED

FERTILITY AND THE ANNUAL ORGY OF

CHLOROPHYL, WHEN THE GREENEST OF

GREENS IS UPON THE LAND.

ALLEN FLETCHER

ALLEN FLETCHER

GLENN PERRY

LARRY KNIVETON

AUTUMN — TIME OF THE
HARVEST, THE SPECTACULAR
DEATH-RITE OF FOLIAGE, AND
THE BITTERSWEET SHORTENING
OF THE DAYS.

LARRY KNIVETON

SEAN MULCAHY

SEAN MULCAHY

LARRY KNIVETON

LARRY KNIVETON

ALLEN FLETCHER

LARRY KNIVETON

GLENN PERRY

SEAN MULCAHY

TROY THOMPSON

LARRY KNIVETON

ERIKA SIDOR

And Spring – miraculous season of regeneration and hope.

PROFILES
OF EXCELLENCE

Following is a close-up look at the corporations, institutions and professional firms in the Central Massachusetts region who have made this book possible. Their stories are arranged by the year these businesses and institutions were founded, and chronicle the commitment these concerns have to their communities.

of inding a bank that will go above and beyond for you at every turn in the road is hard to come by. Customers at TD Banknorth Massachusetts know that this is the kind of high-quality service they receive every day at their hometown bank.

Whoever you are and wherever you are in life, you can count on the bank to go above and beyond to help. TD Banknorth Massachusetts offers virtually every financial service you need from varied banking products for individual needs to meet life's many challenges to a complete offering of commercial services for businesses of all sizes.

TD Banknorth Massachusetts is a $9 billion financial services company and the fourth-largest bank in Massachusetts. The company offers a full range of banking products and services, including retail banking, commercial and consumer lending, residential mortgage lending, asset and investment management products and services in addition to the latest technology for on-line banking, telephone banking and branch banking.

Their customer service philosophy combines the personal attention and local decision-making of a community bank with the strength of the bank's network of financial services. Their approach is to develop partnerships with customers and tailor solutions that are right for them.

Going above and beyond in the community is another way that TD Banknorth differentiates itself as a local community bank. TD Banknorth launched a financial literacy program in Massachusetts designed to help individuals learn more about the basics of banking and ways to manage their money and credit responsibly. Bank employees volunteer their time to teach personal finance, consumer protection and small-business development education to clients of non-profit organizations throughout Massachusetts. Through these programs, the company will work with local non-profit organizations to identify clients who have a need to better understand and feel more comfortable using financial products and services while helping them protect and manage their money in a safe and effective manner.

TD Banknorth employees continue to educate a wide range of residents in the communities it serves, from senior citizens to elementary and high school students, from recent immigrants to families and individuals.

The bank is also committed to charitable giving and strong civic leadership throughout the state. Hundreds of employees at the bank are involved in a variety of volunteer initiatives serving on boards for various organizations and committees, as well as participating in numerous events and fundraisers for non-profit organizations, such as Chambers of Commerce, the United Way and the public schools throughout the area.

Through the bank's financial support and volunteer work, TD Banknorth remains committed to improving the quality of life in the region. We believe it is our corporate responsibility to help shape the future of the community and operate under the guiding principal that good citizenship is also good business.

TD Banknorth Massachusetts has more than 100 years of experience invested in the communities where they work and live. Their strategy is both long-range and locally focused.

The branches of TD Banknorth Massachusetts have served their customers and communities for a century and are recognized for their commitment to personal service, long-term customer relationships and local decision-making and community involvement.

ABOVE: CHRISTOPHER W. BRAMLEY, STATE PRESIDENT AND CEO, TD BANKNORTH

FLETCHER, TILTON & WHIPPLE, P.C.

efore ground was broken for Mechanics Hall, before the first student enrolled at the College of the Holy Cross, before Worcester even became a city, a legal institution was established here that reflected the honesty, industry and civic-mindedness of Worcester's founders.

That legal institution, now known as Fletcher, Tilton & Whipple, P.C., stands today as one of the premier law firms in Central Massachusetts. With a range of traditional and specialty practice areas, the firm has grown with and responded to the changing needs of its community and clients for nearly two centuries.

The law firm's roots reach back to 1822, when Ira Moore Barton, a cousin of Clara Barton, started his law practice in Oxford. He relocated to Worcester in 1834, and in 1845, Barton joined Peter Child Bacon to form Barton and Bacon, the first of many partnerships, mergers and name changes the firm underwent in its long evolution to Fletcher, Tilton & Whipple, P.C.

Many of the firm's attorneys have offered distinguished service to the community and the nation. Barton served as a judge, state representative, state senator and presidential elector; William Swinton Bennett Hopkins commanded a regiment which saw action in the Civil War; Dwight Foster was appointed to the state Supreme Judicial Court in 1866; Thomas Hovey Gage, Jr. served as counselor to Herbert Hoover in the National Food Administration and George Avery White became president of what is now First Allmerica Financial Insurance Co. in 1943.

This tradition of community service has continued through the years. Firm attorneys have served as district attorneys, judges, legislators, mayors of Worcester, chairmen of the Chamber of Commerce and corporators, trustees and officers of a wide variety of civic groups, charities and commissions. "One of the true joys of a community-based practice such as ours is the unparalleled opportunity it affords us to have our clients and our friends be one and the same, much more as the rule than the exception," says Warner S. Fletcher, a director of the firm and trustee of several local foundations.

Fletcher, Tilton & Whipple, P.C., is well-known for its traditional practices, but the firm also has developed specialized practice areas and business approaches. It serves as corporate counsel for more than 1,000 businesses and non-profit organizations, administers the region's largest estate and

trust practice, and has full-service litigation, commercial lending and land use practices, as well as its own title company. Specialty practice areas include environmental, elder and health care, higher education, labor and employment, and immigration law. The firm has managed its growth to maintain a high level of personal attention and utilizes a large, expert paralegal staff to provide quality, cost-efficient legal services.

The practice of law and the city of Worcester have changed dramatically over the last 183 years and Fletcher, Tilton & Whipple, P.C., has remained at the forefront of both. "We're more than just the oldest law firm in Worcester," says Fletcher. "We've established a history of integrity, leadership and excellence, and we are carrying that tradition into the future."

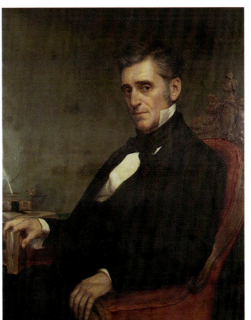

MASSACHUSETTS COLLEGE OF PHARMACY AND HEALTH SCIENCES

of ounded in 1823, the Massachusetts College of Pharmacy and Health Sciences (MCPHS) is the second-oldest college of pharmacy in the United States and the oldest institution of higher education in Boston. Since its founding, the college has dramatically expanded in order to produce the best education possible for health-care leaders across a growing range of disciplines. In 2000, the college opened a second campus in downtown Worcester, and in 2002 a third campus was created in Manchester, New Hampshire.

MCPHS-Worcester offers the area's only academic program devoted to professional pharmacy education — an accelerated, three-year Pharm.D. (Doctor of Pharmacy) program. In addition, an innovative, 16-month Bachelor of Science in Nursing program is available for students who already possess an undergraduate degree in another field. Future baccalaureate programs under consideration for the Worcester campus include Radiologic Sciences and Dental Hygiene.

For students embarking on their clinical rotations, MCPHS-Worcester is ideally located in the heart of a thriving academic and medical community that includes the Worcester Medical Center, Saint Vincent Hospital, UMass Memorial Medical Center and the University of Massachusetts Medical School.

Under the dynamic leadership of President Charles F. Monahan Jr. — who is a Worcester native and graduate of the college — MCPHS has invested more than $40 million in its state-of-the-art campus located in two brilliantly renovated former industrial buildings on Foster Street.

The Henrietta DeBenedictis Building, named in honor of one of the college's most generous philanthropists, is a 60,000-square-foot facility formerly known as The Lowell Building. It features a contemporary instructional pharmacy and compounding laboratory, complete with adjacent patient counseling and sterile products rooms; multi-media auditoriums and classrooms; a health sciences library with electronic audio/video linkages to other MCPHS campuses, as well as other academic and medical libraries; faculty and administrative offices; and a student lounge.

In the fall of 2005, MCPHS-Worcester opened a second campus building located at 25 Foster St. The nine-story Living and Learning Center contains three floors of laboratory and academic space, five floors of student housing and a dramatic ninth-floor

conference center. The five floors of apartment-style housing provide much-needed on-campus living space for 175 students.

MCPHS-Worcester also houses the headquarters of MassMedLine, a state-wide community outreach service providing medication access information and counseling to elderly and under-insured patients. MassMedLine's toll-free hotline is accessible to both the general public and the professional community to assist clients in obtaining free or low-cost medications through the myriad of programs offered by the pharmaceutical industry, as well as state and federal agencies.

MCPHS-Worcester embraces a set of core values that reflect commitment to preparing competent, caring, ethical health professionals and scientists to meet the need for quality health care and cutting-edge knowledge: Learner-centered teaching and

ABOVE: THE COLLEGE'S FIRST BUILDING AT THE CORNER OF FOSTER AND NORWICH STREETS IS NAMED IN HONOR OF HENRIETTA DEBENEDICTIS, A 1931 GRADUATE OF MCPHS AND A PIONEER IN HOSPITAL PHARMACY PRACTICE

student engagement that fosters intellectual vitality, critical thinking and lifelong responsibility for learning and continuing professional development; Honesty, integrity, professionalism and personal responsibility; Respect for diversity and appreciation of cross-cultural perspectives; Adaptability and flexibility in response to the ever-changing external environment; Effective and efficient use of resources to maximize value to those we serve; Excellence and innovation in education, scholarship/research and service, including outreach to the community; A productive, satisfying work and learning environment that is built upon cross-disciplinary and cross-campus collaboration; Integration of the liberal arts and basic sciences with professional studies; Scholarship that contributes to knowledge development, improvement of health sciences education and improvement of health care and health outcomes; and education that fosters development of the whole person.

MCPHS-Worcester provides a unique academic environment to guide and support students toward successful, sustainable careers and leadership in health care. As a private independent institution with a long and distinguished history of specializing in health sciences education, the college offers programs that embody teaching excellence, active scholarship and research, professional service and community outreach. Accordingly, admission to MCPHS-Worcester is competitive and its graduates are highly sought-after by employers throughout the region and the country.

WORCESTER ACADEMY

ounded in 1834, Worcester Academy is the oldest independent school in Central Massachusetts. A co-ed urban day and boarding school for grades 6 to 12 and postgraduates, the Academy has served generations of families who value its "student-centered" tradition. Among its 640 boys and girls are students representing 16 different nations. Its Web address is *www.worcesteracademy.org.*

The Academy's stated mission is to prepare students for college and later life through a "comprehensive program of academics, athletics, the arts and service to the community." Its motto is *"Achieve the Honorable."*

Established as the Worcester County Manual Labor High School in 1834, the Academy first opened its doors as "a school for the education of youth in languages, arts and sciences; for promoting habits of industry and economy; and for inculcating the principles of piety and virtue."

In 1846 the school officially became Worcester Academy; 23 years later it moved from Lincoln Square to its present Union Hill location at 81 Providence St. And in 1882, the Academy welcomed legendary Principal Dr. Daniel Webster Abercrombie, who built most of school's important buildings.

In 1974, the school resumed the admission of girls after a hiatus of 86 years. The Middle School was opened in 1987, followed by the addition of sixth grade in 1996.

The Academy campus blends modern and 19th-century architecture. In keeping with the British model of campus design, most of the buildings face the campus green, also known as "The Quad." Six of the Academy's buildings are on the National Register of Historic Places. Additionally, Warner Theater's Ross Auditorium, the first movie theater ever built on a school campus (1931), has undergone extensive renovations to restore it to its original grandeur.

Along with the main campus, the Academy maintains the Gaskill Field athletic complex, the nearby Alumni House and the New Balance Fields on Stafford Street.

Times have changed since the Worcester County Manual Labor High School, and so has Worcester Academy — but, as in 1834, the school remains committed to providing its students with a solid real-world education.

Today, with a student/teacher ratio of 7 to 1, the Academy challenges students with a classic college-preparatory curriculum taught by accomplished faculty — all the while making use of the most advanced educational technology and the advantages of the school's city setting. The Academy also believes that there are many important life-lessons to be learned outside of the classroom: in its five- and seven-day boarding programs, in the art studio and on stage, on its athletic fields, and in serving the community around them.

Some of Worcester Academy's notable alumni include: Edward Davis Jones (1873), co-founder of Dow Jones; Gilbert Hovey Grosvenor (1893), founder of National Geographic; Charles Merrill (1904), founder of Merrill Lynch; American songwriter Cole Porter (1909); Arnold Hiatt (1944), chairman of the Stride Rite Foundation; Arnold Lehman (1962), director of the Brooklyn Museum of Art; James P. McGovern (1977), U.S. Representative, Third District, Massachusetts; and Rick Carlisle (1979), head coach of the Indiana Pacers.

LEFT: WARNER THEATER'S ROSS AUDITORIUM, THE JEWEL OF ALL OF THE ACADEMY'S HISTORIC BUILDINGS. BUILT IN THE 1930S FROM A DONATION BY WARNER BROTHERS STUDIO PRESIDENT HARRY WARNER, THE BUILDING IS NAMED IN MEMORY OF WARNER'S SON LEWIS, CLASS OF 1928

BELOW: WALKER HALL, A BUSTLING HIVE OF CAMPUS ACTIVITY, HAS AN IVY-COVERED EXTERIOR OF POSTCARD-LIKE BEAUTY. INSIDE ARE ADMINISTRATIVE OFFICES, THE ANDES PIT THEATER, CLASSROOMS AND A SOARING ART STUDIO BRIMMING WITH NATURAL LIGHT

COLLEGE OF THE HOLY CROSS

Established in 1843 as New England's first Catholic college, the College of the Holy Cross is renowned for its mentoring-based, liberal arts education in the Jesuit tradition. An exclusively undergraduate institution, Holy Cross assures its students of a highly personalized intellectual experience. The college integrates faith and knowledge with an emphasis on service to others, offers many innovative academic programs and cocurricular options and fosters scholar athletes.

Much more than a place for career preparation, Holy Cross challenges and stimulates its students to discover their gifts and sense of purpose in the world. This process occurs as the college's 2,700 students and 295 faculty members gather in classrooms, labs and studios to explore the liberal arts together — and to carry that spirit of exploration through the life of the college and beyond.

Academically, Holy Cross consistently rates highly in surveys conducted by independent college guides, both nationwide and among other liberal-arts schools. Its graduation and alumni-giving rates are among the best in the nation, attesting to the fact that Holy Cross students are actively engaged by their learning experiences and remain highly connected and supportive as alumni.

Holy Cross students are regularly awarded prestigious Fulbright and Watson Fellowships to study, conduct research and teach abroad. The college ranks in the top 3% in the number of its students going on to earn doctorates, and its graduates are admitted to medical school at a rate more than twice the national average.

Holy Cross faculty, virtually all of whom hold a Ph.D., are recognized not only as teachers and mentors, but also for their scholarly research, publications and creative work. Their many grant and fellowship awards support innovative programs at Holy Cross as well as in the Worcester Public Schools that enhance student learning and teaching opportunities.

In keeping with the Jesuit call to be "men and women for others," Holy Cross students, faculty and staff have long been active contributors to the betterment of the Worcester community. This commitment manifests in several community service programs, the largest of which is Student Programs for Urban Development. Sponsored by the Chaplain's Office, SPUD consists of 25 outreach programs and has 350 active student volunteers. SPUD activities include serving meals to the homeless, tutoring students in the public schools, visiting with nursing home residents, cleaning the city's streets and parks, refurbishing shelters, and counseling domestic

violence victims. Holy Cross employees and students also coordinate and donate to several annual food, fund and clothing drives to benefit needy Worcester residents.

Athletically, Holy Cross has a storied and very proud tradition of excellence. The college is a founding member of the Patriot League, an NCAA Division I league that emphasizes academic as well as athletic achievement. The Music, Visual and Theatre Arts programs at Holy Cross are also widely renowned, and offer many shows and performances available for the public to attend.

Holy Cross and Worcester have enjoyed a strong partnership for more than 160 years and, together, are committed to providing an excellent environment in which to live and learn.

PHOTOS/CHRISTOPHER NAVIN

CITY OF WORCESTER

Welcome to Worcester — *A City on the Move!*
With 6 million people living within a 50-mile radius, unique opportunities exist in Worcester for dynamic business growth and quality residential living. The city, founded in 1848, is centrally located in the heart of the Commonwealth, and was once among the pre-eminent manufacturing cities in the nation. Today, Worcester is still setting the pace, as it did more than 100 years ago. Worcester has transformed itself into a leader in advanced manufacturing, information technology, biotechnology, health care and medical research.

Worcester's landscape blends impressive mills and diverse architecture with community-oriented neighborhoods and inviting green spaces. Worcester's rich history of immigrant populations is evident in its diverse neighborhoods and cultural fabric. Today, that tradition continues as Worcester welcomes new residents to live and prosper; and celebrates its continuing diversity through community festivals and events throughout the year.

There is always something happening in Worcester. From world-renowned museums and concert halls to regionally lauded theaters, galleries, performing arts venues and festivals, Worcester truly is the city where culture shines. Worcester is the proud home to professional baseball with the Worcester Tornadoes, offering families and baseball fans of all ages exciting and affordable fun. In their inaugural season, the Tornadoes captured the Can-Am League championship. Likewise the city's abundance of restaurants and eateries ensure that, whether you are looking for a five-star dining experience or simply a quick bite to eat, Worcester has something to suit every appetite. Worcester also features numerous neighborhood retail centers, as well as countless specialty shops.

Worcester is recognized throughout the Commonwealth for its innovative development and public safety programs, creative and effective public-private partnerships at the local, state and federal levels, and bold vision and leadership. Worcester and its leadership stand firmly committed to aggressively moving these projects forward from vision to reality and to positioning our city as a flourishing municipality with an extraordinary quality of life that is attractive to residents, businesses and visitors.

With several major development projects on the horizon that will have tremendous economic impact, the city is on the threshold of a new dawn. These projects and initiatives will transform Worcester's skyline and reverberate throughout our neighborhoods. The signature CitySquare project, the new

Hilton Garden Inn and Regional Justice Center, and redevelopment projects such as Gateway Park and Kilby-Gardner-Hammond will have major impact on our neighborhoods and stimulate the remediation of contaminated brownfield sites into productive re-use. These are but a few of the myriad key development projects which will further strengthen Worcester's position as a true destination and ensure its attractiveness and livability for generations to come.

This truly is an exciting time for the city of Worcester. Many dynamic initiatives and projects are under way which will create a favorable environment for development and enhance the quality of life for our residents. This significant and progressive agenda includes major investments in our downtown and improvements to our extensive transportation network; a new, state-of-the-art vocational school with an innovative and integrated curriculum preparing today's students for tomorrow's workforce; and an increasing number of public/private partnerships that have resulted in new initiatives that will benefit the entire city. These initiatives, coupled with an exceptional primary and secondary school system with nationally acclaimed programs; nine outstanding colleges and universities in the city and several more throughout the region that produce intellectual capital second to none; a competitively priced housing market; a growing biotechnology, health care and medical industry; and a skilled and highly educated workforce, combine to make Worcester an exceptional city with a brilliant future.

City Manager Michael V. O'Brien invites you to experience this *City on the Move.* Find out for yourself what makes Worcester, Massachusetts, such a wonderful place to live, to work and to visit.

ABOVE: THE WORCESTER CITY HALL CLOCK TOWER

BELOW: HISTORIC UNION STATION INTERMODAL TRANSPORTATION CENTER

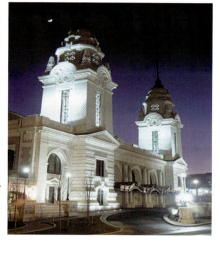

SOUTHBRIDGE SAVINGS BANK

outhbridge Savings Bank first opened its doors in 1848 to the first depositor, Fanny Richardson. In August of the same year the bank granted its first mortgage to local blacksmith Charles E. Cady. The group of founders, which included prominent industrialists in town as well as civic and political leaders, decided to open a mutual savings institution that would pay depositors dividends and provide a means for individuals to own homes. Ever since that day, the bank has supported the local community in their personal and professional endeavors.

During the next century, the bank grew as the community began to grow and prosper. Many people came to the city from the country looking for employment and Southbridge Savings Bank helped fund new businesses and homes. By the beginning of the 20th century, the inventions of electricity and automobiles brought much more growth to Southbridge, bringing the total population up to 10,000. By the time World War I began, the bank's assets had risen to nearly $3 million, which mirrored the growth of the times. With business booming in the 1920s, industry and businesses began expanding. The bank, however maintained its traditional policy of "merit before magnitude" and this philosophy saved many Southbridge Savings Bank customers from the disastrous events resulting from the stock market crash in 1929.

During the ensuing 40 years, the bank continued to expand and in 1972 the Southbridge Savings Bank opened its first branch in Sturbridge; another opened soon after in Charlton in 1976.

Through the recession of the mid 1970s, the bank maintained its standard of remaining profitable even during the downturn of the economy, which affected many persons throughout the country.

In the 1980s, Southbridge Savings Bank expanded its services again after joining with the Federal Deposit Insurance Corporation (FDIC) and opened another branch at The Fair Shopping Plaza in Southbridge. The bank began offering innovative services, including automobile loans, debit cards and, with the opening of a new branch at the Big Y in Spencer in 1996, the convenience of in-store banking. Since that time seven more branches have been added, offering convenient banking and innovative products to 10 communities from Amherst to Worcester. With the opening of the Palmer branch in 2005, the bank now offers 13 full-service locations throughout Central and Western Massachusetts, including seven in-store branches that are open extended hours, seven days a week.

As Southbridge Savings Bank looks toward a new century of operation, the vision set forth by its founders in 1848 carries on. By staying true to the tradition of leadership, trustworthiness and service, the bank will continue to earn the loyalty of customers while it recommits to remaining a strong, hometown bank.

WORCESTER POLYTECHNIC INSTITUTE

The nation's third-oldest private independent technological university, and a national university consistently ranked among the top 60 such institutions by *U.S. News & World Report*, WPI has been a part of the fabric of the Worcester community since its founding in 1865 as the Worcester County Free Institute of Industrial Science.

The university's founders include John Boynton, a successful tinware manufacturer from Templeton, who foresaw the impact the Industrial Revolution would have on life and work in New England. With his life's savings of $100,000, he established a new type of school to educate young people to become leaders in engineering, manufacturing and commerce. Stephen Salisbury II, Worcester's most prominent business leader, gave the school 6.5 acres of land near Salisbury Street — the nucleus of today's 80-acre campus — and Worcester industrialist Ichabod Washburn donated a model manufacturing facility where students could apply the theories they learned in the classroom.

That balance between theory and practice has been the hallmark of a WPI education and is embodied today in an innovative approach to undergraduate education. A rigorous classroom and laboratory curriculum immerses students in the fundamentals of science, mathematics, engineering and the liberal arts and is enriched by real-world projects that enable students to put what they learn into practice: in the humanities and arts; in understanding how science, technology and social issues intersect in today's world; and in original design and research that gives them professional experience in their chosen disciplines.

WPI's traditional New England campus is well-designed to fulfill the university's mission of discovering new knowledge and preparing young people for success in life and work. Its modern research facilities include atomic force microscopes, medical imaging laboratories, a supercomputer and a satellite navigation lab. Along with a host of multimedia classrooms and lecture halls, students have access to an outstanding array of academic and project facilities — from a bioprocess lab, to a manufacturing design studio, to computer music labs, to a "little theater" facility. WPI's exceptional computer and networking infrastructure has won the university a number of "most-connected campus" designations. The gleaming 71,000-square-foot Campus Center is the heart of the campus, while the new Bartlett Center offers a

spectacular welcome to prospective students and their families. In the planning stages are a state-of-the-art sports and recreation complex and the transformation of WPI's library into a 21st-century information center.

WPI's award-winning Global Perspective Program, one of the most comprehensive and highly regarded global studies programs in the nation, provides a unique experience for students to be educated around the world. About two-thirds complete their required projects off campus; nearly half travel outside the United States to a network of

ABOVE: A STUDENT PROJECT TEAM IN VENICE, ONE OF MORE THAN 20 SITES IN WPI's GLOBAL PERSPECTIVE PROGRAM

BELOW: SOME OF THE TECHNOLOGY THAT HAS EARNED WPI A NUMBER OF "MOST CONNECTED CAMPUS" DESIGNATIONS

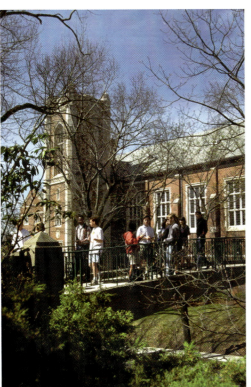

ABOVE: THE EARLE BRIDGE AND, BEHIND IT, ALDEN MEMORIAL, LANDMARKS ON WPI'S TRADITIONAL NEW ENGLAND CAMPUS BELOW: MODERN TEACHING AND RESEARCH LABORATORIES SUPPORT MORE THAN 50 UNDERGRADUATE AND GRADUATE DEGREE PROGRAMS

more than 20 project centers on five continents. Students spend seven intensive weeks — not in the classroom, but in the field — solving important problems for agencies and organizations around the globe.

The university's network of project centers also gives students opportunities in their own backyard. The Worcester Community Project Center focuses on projects that benefit the local community and is just one component in WPI's overall commitment to forging a strong and enduring relationship with the city of Worcester. Currently, WPI is playing an active role in the economic development of the city and the region through its involvement in Gateway Park, an 11-acre former brownfield site being redeveloped as a mixed-use, life sciences-based campus by a partnership between WPI and the Worcester Business Development Corporation.

Today, most of WPI's academic departments offer advanced degree programs that can be pursued on a full- or part-time basis, on campus or through distance learning. The university offers more than 50 degree programs, from a bachelor's degree to a Ph.D. Through its graduate research programs, WPI faculty and students, working in more than 30 research laboratories, centers and institutes, are engaged in groundbreaking work in a broad range of fields — including advanced materials processing, aerospace engineering, fire protection engineering, medical imaging, nanotechnology, satellite navigation and wireless technology. WPI's Metal Processing Institute is the largest industry/university alliance in North America, and its Bioengineering Institute has received major research awards from the federal government to develop medical technologies that will benefit society and spur regional economic growth.

WPI, its faculty and its students have won significant recognition through the years. It was the only technological university among the 16 national Leadership Institutions selected by the Association of American Colleges and Universities to serve as a model of outstanding practices in liberal education. In the National Survey of Student Engagement, WPI ranked No. 1 out of 33 doctoral-intensive universities for "student-faculty interactions," a measure of the quality and quantity of time faculty spend with undergraduates. WPI's faculty includes 11 Fulbright Scholars, more than 40 fellows of professional societies and 17 recipients of the CAREER Award, the National Science Foundation's most prestigious honor for young faculty members.

Universities measure their success in many ways — by the quality of the students they attract, by the accomplishments of their faculties, and by the support they receive from their constituencies. By all of these measures, WPI has been highly successful. But the best measure of its effectiveness is the success of its graduates. Over the years, WPI alumni have invented, designed and manufactured technologies that have changed our lives. They have founded and run myriad companies, designed and erected buildings, dams and bridges, and fashioned great networks of railways, highways, waterways and power lines. They have made scientific discoveries and explored uncharted territory — both physical and metaphorical. With their ideas, their imagination, their knowledge, their creativity and their leadership, they helped build our modern world and are at work today on the world of tomorrow.

For more information about WPI, visit www.wpi.edu.

WEBSTER FIVE CENTS SAVINGS BANK

Many banks *serve* their community. At Webster Five, we're *part* of our community.

Since opening for business on August 10, 1868, Webster Five has played an integral role in the development of our region. Supporting local neighborhoods and providing personal, one-on-one financial services to local residents through every life stage was our mission more than 135 years ago. And it still is today.

Here, old-fashioned service is our way of life. We treat our customers with professionalism and respect the way we'd want to be treated and we always greet them with a smile. At the same time, we also offer our community the latest and most advanced financial products and services. In fact, Webster Five was one of the first local banks to offer totally free checking, and we also led the way with on-line banking and enhanced technology — all to make your banking easier.

And, while many local banks have been bought by or have merged with out-of-state mega-banks, Webster Five has remained dedicated to high-quality, face-to-face service at every one of our branch locations. It's the best of both worlds — caring and friendly old-school service combined with cutting-edge solutions and delivery systems. All from local professionals who can make decisions and who truly care about your satisfaction and well-being.

Webster Five has maintained steady growth and stable management throughout its history. And, in 2005, we received a five-star rating from Bauer Financial Reports — the highest rating a bank can receive among its peers.

While offering an array of diversified financial services to serve *every* financial need in our community — including personal banking, mortgages, business banking, cash management and investment services (through Raymond James Financial Services Inc.) — Webster Five is still committed to reinvesting profits back to the people we serve. That's why, in 1995, we developed the Webster Five Foundation, a non-profit fund to serve worthwhile community-related causes. Since the Foundation's inception, Webster Five has distributed more than $820,000 in charitable contributions to non-profit organizations. We also participate in the Massachusetts Saving

Makes 'Cents' Program, an educational program designed to teach the principles of banking in the classroom.

The bank's headquarters is located on Thompson Road in Webster, with offices in Auburn, Dudley, Oxford, Webster and Worcester. In 2002, we continued our long-term commitment to the Worcester community by opening our third location in the city, at 200 Commercial St. With expansion a part of our strategic goals, a new branch will open in Shrewsbury in 2006. The bank also opened a state-of-the-art Operations Center in Auburn to consolidate support services in one location, allowing us to serve customers more efficiently.

For more than 135 years, our bank has been a model of success. And our future looks even more promising. Webster Five is truly unique among other banks. Here, high-tech meets high-touch. And we value people as much as any asset in our vault.

Webster Five. We're different. We're better. Believe it.

ABOVE: WEBSTER FIVE CENTS SAVINGS BANK, MAIN OFFICE, WEBSTER, MASSACHUSETTS
BELOW: RICHARD C. LAWTON, PRESIDENT/CEO, WEBSTER FIVE CENTS SAVINGS BANK

WORCESTER STATE COLLEGE

lthough students come from all over the world to study at Worcester State College, 94% are home-grown — citizens of the Commonwealth. For more than 130 years, Worcester State College has supported the educational and career aspirations of high-achieving, highly motivated students from all walks of life. From its earliest days as the Worcester Normal School right up to the present, the college has remained committed to the ideal of building a better society through quality, affordable higher education. As a public institution, it has set high standards — to make a superior education available to the many, not just the few.

It all began on September 11, 1874, when the state opened a Normal School in Worcester that would educate women to become teachers. The first graduating class numbered only 10. From these humble origins, Worcester State College has emerged as a dynamic, four-year liberal arts and sciences college with more than 5,400 students. Similarly, the college's facilities have grown from one Gothic structure to nine major buildings situated on a beautiful, leafy, 58-acre campus in the residential West Side of Worcester. With their required laptop computers, students enjoy 24/7 access to the network in a wireless campus environment.

In response to the region's economic interests, Worcester State College, under the leadership of President Janelle C. Ashley, has expanded its degree programs to include biomedical sciences and the health professions. More than half of the college's students are non-traditional and enroll in the Division of Continuing Education to obtain a degree, improve their career skills or change careers. Offering both bachelor's and master's degrees, with a full range of academic majors, Worcester State College was named a "Best Northeastern College" by *The Princeton Review*.

The Graduate School confers master's degrees in education, management, non-profit management, biotechnology, health care administration, speech-language pathology and occupational therapy. Provisional certification programs are offered in early childhood, elementary and middle school/secondary education.

Distinguished faculty include Fulbright Scholars, National Science Foundation Fellows, American Council on Education (ACE) Fellows, and published authors. With more than 170 full-time professors and moderate-size classes, students are afforded personal interaction with their professors.

One of the cornerstones of the college's mission is public service. The strongest exam-

ple of community outreach and engagement is Worcester State College's Latino Education Institute (LEI), which has made a significant mark in the lives of hundreds of Latino students in Worcester.

With an employee base of more than 500, and a commitment to service, the college's positive impact on the community and deep connection to the economic and cultural resources of Central Massachusetts are strongly evident with 80% of the college's 28,000 alumni living and working in the Commonwealth.

ABOVE: THE KALYAN K. GHOSH SCIENCE AND TECHNOLOGY CENTER PROVIDES SOPHISTICATED LABORATORY CLASSROOMS AND EQUIPMENT
LEFT: THE DIVERSITY OF THE COLLEGE IS CELEBRATED EVERY YEAR WITH THE MULTICULTURAL FESTIVAL

POLAR BEVERAGES

olar Beverages is the largest privately owned, independent soft-drink bottler in the United States. Polar traces its history to 1882 and the establishment of the J.G. Bieberbach Company. This company manufactured seltzer and ginger ale, imported mineral water and was a wholesaler of alcoholic beverages. Prior to coming to Worcester, Bieberbach, who immigrated to New York City from Germany at the request of The Shafer Brewing Company, was the first to brew Pilsner beer for consumption in the United States.

In 1901 Dennis M. Crowley, the great grandfather of the present owners of Polar Beverages, founded D. M. Crowley & Co., a wholesale and retail liquor business with a division called Polar Spring Water. The top-selling product of the day was "Crowley's Ball Brook Straight Whiskey." Dennis, also known as "Boss Crowley," was a second-generation American. Shortly after founding the company, Polar acquired the Bieberbach company. For the next 50 years the company was known as the Bieber Polar Ginger Ale Company.

Polar Beverages' corporate headquarters are centrally located at the crossroads of routes I-290, I-495, I-190 and the Massachusetts Turnpike. This site is ideally located to service our primary markets in the Northeast. Polar Beverages' Worcester plant is 550,000 square feet, houses five dedicated carbonated-beverage lines, a spring-water production line and a post-and-premix line.

To service its continuing growth, Polar has distribution centers in Worcester, Avon and Holyoke; Milford, Connecticut; and Newburg, New York. Polar also has an extensive network of exclusive distributors that represent the company in its remaining marketplace.

Polar's business segments include the company's flagship "Polar" brand, franchise national brands, new age spring waters and private label brands. Over the last two decades, Polar has made 20 nationally branded acquisitions. These purchases have focused on Cadbury Schweppes PLC's corporate brands. These include 7Up, Sunkist, A&W , Royal Crown, Snapple and Nantucket Nectars.

In December, 1995, Polar acquired Adirondack Beverages of Scotia, New York. Adirondack is Polar's second production facility, with more than 650,000 square feet of space. The Adirondack plant also has

four dedicated carbonated-beverage lines and a water production line. Adirondack produces a full flavor line of carbonated beverages under the Adirondack, Waist Watcher and Clear 'n' Natural labels in addition to retail branded product, as well as co-packing product for other beverage companies.

Polar Beverages has a long established reputation for quality, strong customer relationships and brand loyalty. This has been accomplished by the continued acquisitions of established name brands and the development and innovation of new products and packaging as opportunities are presented to satisfy the ever-changing tastes of its customers.

LEFT: POLAR'S LARGER-THAN-LIFE "CANS" ON TOP OF THE WORCESTER PLANT
BELOW: POLAR PRODUCES 4 MILLION 12-OUNCE SERVINGS A DAY IN THEIR PLANTS

WACHUSETT MOUNTAIN

Wachusett Mountain Association, a sister company of Polar Beverages, has been owned by the Crowley family since 1969. Wachusett Mountain has a long history of providing great skiing for the region; and since the late 1880s, when the first hotel was constructed on the summit, Wachusett Mountain has attracted tourists from around the world.

The name "Wachusett" is the Algonquin Indian word for "The Great Hill," and true to its name, the mountain offers outstanding and fun skiing for skiers of all levels.

The mountain boasts 22 trails with 108 skiable acres. The trails include skiing for all skill levels, including: novice (30% of the trails), intermediate (40%) and advanced (30%).

There are eight lifts with an uphill capacity of more than 9,200 skiers per hour, and this includes the only two high-speed quad chair lifts in Massachusetts.

Wachusett Mountain also features a long tradition of skiing in Central Massachusetts. In the 1930s, the Civilian Corps cut the first skiing trails — Pine Hill Trail in 1934 and Balance Rock Trail in 1937. The first lifts were added in the 1960s — the Oxbow T-bar in 1960 and the West T-bar in 1962, which was the longest T-bar in New England, measuring 3,800 feet.

More than 1 million people visit the mountain year-round, with more than 40% of that number visiting the Wachusett Mountain State Reservation in the summer and fall.

Wachusett Mountain also offers a variety of services for skiers and their families. They have a ski and snowboard school, which is dedicated to providing a fun learning experience in a variety of programs for all abilities. The mountain has the largest ski school in Massachusetts, with 200 instructors. More than 10,000 beginner-ski school lessons are taught annually.

Wachusett Mountain also offers children's programs called Polar Kids, Polar Den Club and Polar Playground. The Polar Cub Nursery is available seven days a week for babysitting children three months to four years of age.

Wachusett Mountain has the No. 1 NASTAR program in New England and ranks in the Top 10 in the United States. NASTAR is the world's largest recreational ski-racing program. Wachusett also has one of the largest Corporate Night Race League programs in the country, with approximately 200 racers participating for eight weeks during the winter.

The Mountain also offers snowboarding, with plenty of diverse terrain for all abilities, including a half-pipe and alpine park. The Mountainside Ski & Sport Shop has the latest snowboard equipment and

apparel, and the Wachusett Mountain Ski School also offers a variety of learn-to-snowboard programs.

Wachusett has won many national awards for its varied services. In the winter of 2003-2004, Wachusett Mountain earned high honors from *Ski* magazine for its access, weather, service, on-mountain food and family programs. The mountain ranked in the Top 10 for the East's best ski resorts in 10 different categories, in addition to ranking No. 10 overall.

They have also received numerous environmental awards, including their most recent honor, the 2003 Silver Eagle Award for Wildlife and Habitat Protection.

ABOVE: NORTH FACE VIEW OF WACHUSETT MOUNTAIN

BELOW: ALL TRAILS ARE LIT FOR NIGHT SKIING

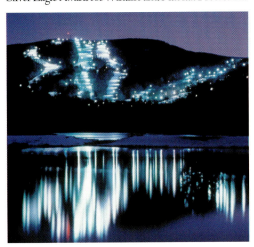

WORCESTER REGIONAL CHAMBER OF COMMERCE

s the largest Chamber in New England, the Worcester Regional Chamber of Commerce is dedicated to enhancing the region's economic prosperity and the vitality of its business community. The mission of the Chamber is to support existing businesses and promote economic development in the Worcester region by being a bold, strong, articulate and effective advocate. The Chamber believes that a strong business community is a catalyst to a dynamic area in which to live.

WORCESTER IS OPEN FOR BUSINESS

The Worcester Regional Chamber of Commerce represents thousands of members through public policy advocacy and economic development initiatives that create balanced regional growth. The Chamber delivers valuable programming, support services and growth opportunities to our membership. Extensive networking opportunities are available through a wide variety of events, along with valuable programs that assist businesses — large and small — to operate successfully.

The Chamber's roots trace back to December 1873, when a group of prominent businessmen established the Worcester Business Exchange. It was the state's first business organization. In February 1875, the state officially recognized the organization, which was renamed the Worcester Board of Trade. In 1913, the organization merged with the Merchant's Association to become the Chamber of Commerce.

As the third-largest city in New England with more than $1 billion in economic development initiatives under way in the downtown area — Worcester is truly the epicenter of the region. Central Massachusetts — often referred to as the "Heart of the Commonwealth" — is a region that is rich in culture, education and history, as well as a bustling center for business, industry and commerce.

In recent years, the Chamber has greatly expanded its role as a regional organization with the affiliations of the Auburn, Blackstone Valley, Holden Area, Tri-Community Area and Webster Dudley Oxford Chambers of Commerce. Addressing the needs and concerns of businesses as a regional, unified voice is an effective way of promoting the region to enhance the quality of each individual city and town. Just a few of the reasons that companies have remained and prospered in the region include a strong workforce, economic vitality and an exceptional quality of life.

Through the years, the Chamber has enjoyed a record of success in working to attract industry and in recognizing local businesses for their achievements and contributions to the region. This continues to be the Chamber's focus today.

The Chamber offers everything you need to grow your own business: economic development, site search assistance, business assistance, public policy advocacy along with networking and educational opportunities.

The Chamber's Business Resource Assistance Center allows members to access a wide range of financial and technical assistance programs and services, at one central location — a convenient and valuable service for those business owners, entrepreneurs and developers whose time is precious.

Much of the Chamber's strength lies with its volunteers — local business people who promote the Chamber and the region through volunteer activities, committees and events.

Keeping in step with the times, and possessing a strong ability to bring business together, is at the core of the Chamber's success. Through its many member programs, services and events, and maintaining the vital role it plays in shaping the regional economy, the Worcester Regional Chamber of Commerce fulfills its mission to it members and to the community.

ABOVE: (L-R) MAIN STREET OFFICE BUILDINGS, INTERIOR OF UNION STATION, REGIONAL JUSTICE CENTER UNDER CONSTRUCTION, WORCESTER REGIONAL AIRPORT TERMINAL, COMMUTER RAIL STATION

A more-than-200-year-old institution is not immune to occasional lapses in local memory.

What local college now offers more than 20 bachelor's degrees, and is expanding into graduate studies, yet is still often referred to as a junior college?

What college has a co-op educational experience that pre-dates Northeastern University's? ...Is popularly thought of as a women's college but was never a women's college? ... Is one of a handful that runs its own veterinary clinic that's not part of a separate veterinary school? ... Is often still called "Becker's," a name it has not used since 1926?

The answer to all of the above is: Becker College.

Unique class offerings and a hands-on professional-practitioner approach have earned Becker a national reputation for career-focused academics. Students are engaged with the community through coursework and service projects and choose from more than 30 academic programs, including extensive adult learning options.

With a campus in the Elm Park neighborhood of Worcester and on the Town Common in Leicester, Becker is steward to some of the most historic properties in Central Massachusetts. Becker is also proud to be associated with some luminaries of American history. John Hancock and Samuel Adams signed incorporation papers for the college.

Eli Whitney, inventor of the cotton gin, was a member of the first graduating class in 1788. Harry G. Stoddard, Worcester industrialist, graduated in 1893. J. Lee Richmond of The Worcesters pitched the first perfect game in professional baseball on the site of Becker College in Worcester.

Becker College President Ken Zirkle, Ed.D., says: "The dedicated and caring faculty and staff at Becker are committed to the education of the total student. They prepare our students for the challenges of a fast-paced, ever-changing world and are focused on keeping up-to-date with the newest developments in their fields."

Becker has hosted forums and symposiums, bringing such figures to campus as Dr. Jane Goodall, Dr. Hunter "Patch" Adams and U.S. Poet Laureate Stanley Kunitz. Becker is not afraid to tackle complex social issues, either. With one of the strongest nursing programs in the state, the college provided a forum for leaders in government, health care and education to discuss solutions to a serious nursing shortage.

New programs are added to educate today's traditional and adult students. Business meets veterinary science in an equine studies program. Information technology, design and liberal arts faculty join forces to produce computer game designers and programmers in the interactive entertainment bachelor's degree program. The Becker Hawks NCAA Division III athletics program includes football, lacrosse and hockey teams. With accelerated degree programs at locations throughout the state and courses available online, Becker is even breaking free of the brick-and-mortar campus.

Becker serves more than 1,600 students with a full-time enrollment of more than 1,100 from 18 states and 12 countries. A student/faculty ratio of 15-1 allows for dynamic exchange in the classroom and mentoring relationships that last beyond graduation.

Becker Trustee and Class of 1964 member Colleen C. Barrett, now president and COO of Southwest Airlines, says: "My professors at Becker were great, and one professor in particular had a profound impact on me. When I began working, I discovered [my boss] ran his law practice the same team-oriented, mentoring way that wonderful professor at Becker ran his class. Most of my leadership style, behavior and philosophy today is very consistent with what I learned from the very get-go and Becker College was an essential part of that."

ABOVE: AS A DYNAMIC AND EVOLVING INSTITUTION OF HIGHER LEARNING, BECKER COLLEGE PROVIDES A CRITICAL SERVICE

FOR MANY FIRST-GENERATION COLLEGE STUDENTS, AND STUDENTS WHO VALUE PERSONAL ATTENTION, BECKER OFFERS THE OPPORTUNITY AND GUIDANCE FOR A SUCCESSFUL PROFESSIONAL CAREER

CLARK UNIVERSITY

Clark University has a long and distinguished reputation as an institution for academic excellence and intellectual innovation. Throughout the last 120 years, many Clark faculty, students and alumni have left their mark on the world.

Founded by Jonas Clark in 1887, Clark was the nation's first all-graduate institution. The university's first president, G. Stanley Hall, founded the American Psychological Association and earned the first Ph.D. in psychology in the United States, at Harvard. Clark has since played a prominent role in the development of psychology as a distinguished discipline in this country. In his only speaking engagement in the United States, Sigmund Freud delivered his famous "Clark Lectures" at the university in 1909.

Clark is also well-known throughout the country and around the world for its outstanding Graduate School of Geography and undergraduate geography programs. Clark has granted more Ph.D.s in geography than any other school in the nation, and four Clark geography faculty members — an impressive number — are members of the National Academy of Science. The George Perkins Marsh Institute was the first research center created to study the human dimensions of global environmental change. In recent years, Clark has had a major impact on the widespread use of Geographic Information Systems technology through the IDRISI software developed by the Clark Labs; and the university is gaining a worldwide reputation for its International Development, Community, and Environment programs.

JONAS CLARK HALL

Hall could be credited with inaugurating Clark's reputation for nurturing pioneering individuals who aren't afraid to challenge conventional wisdom to discover new ways of looking at the world. He was the first to develop the concept of adolescence as a separate stage of human development. Other notable researchers on the Clark faculty have included Robert Goddard, the father of the space age and inventor of rocket technology; and A.A. Michelson, who first calculated the speed of light. Clark faculty and alumni first developed and measured the wind-chill factor, invented intelligence testing and three-dimensional film, conducted the research that led to the birth control pill and shaped what were once burgeoning fields of study — anthropology, film and jazz criticism, animal behavior and child development, just to name a few.

Today's Clark students and faculty share their predecessors' penchant for pursuing new ideas and creating positive change. With the university's active-learning approach to higher education, undergraduates, graduate students and faculty are working together to solve real-world problems. In the university's science labs, for example, students and faculty are researching ways to create new materials, contributing important genetic information

to genome projects, and helping to find new ways to fight disease. The same kind of collaboration is developing new knowledge in the social sciences, arts and humanities. At Clark, undergraduates have unique opportunities to pursue their scholarly and creative interests. With support from a variety of special fellowships, Clark students create film and fine art, and conduct research around the world in a variety of disciplines — all in the interest of discovering something new.

Clark takes its role in the world seriously, supporting students and faculty in their engagement with the local and global community. Clark's leadership role in the University Park Partnership, a revitalization effort in Worcester's Main South neighborhood, demonstrates the university's commitment to social action while creating many opportunities for students and faculty to make meaningful connections with the community beyond its campus. If Worcester needs help solving a problem or examining an issue, Clark students and faculty are there. Most recently, they have helped the city with issues related to economic development, education and urban revitalization. Beyond Worcester, Clark students and faculty can be found around the world, conducting research and using new knowledge to help communities develop successfully or heal from disasters, such as the tsunami in Southeast Asia or the genocide in Rwanda.

With its hands-on approach to learning and commitment to social action and change, Clark attracts an eclectic mix of students, faculty and staff from all corners of the globe, who represent a wide range of backgrounds, interests and ethnicities. Clark celebrates its intercultural community and has a curriculum that is global in its view. All of these factors contribute to Clark's distinctive and vibrant learning environment, which continues to nurture those pioneering individuals who will change our understanding of the world in years to come.

ABOVE: THE ALDEN ATRIUM IN CLARK'S LASRY CENTER FOR BIOSCIENCE
RIGHT: CLARK PHYSICS PROFESSOR CHRISTOPHER LANDEE DOES A PHYSICS DEMONSTRATION FOR HIS STUDENTS

SAINT VINCENT HOSPITAL

The futuristic expanse of glass, brick and terraced greenery in the heart of downtown Worcester that has been home to Saint Vincent Hospital since 2000 is a testament to the hospital's continued evolution as a pioneer in regional health care. At a time when most medical facilities were cutting resources amid economic challenges, Saint Vincent Hospital built the state-of-the-art medical center to meet its expanding needs as an acute-care hospital and cutting-edge teaching facility. Now, the hospital has launched a new chapter in its 100-year history, marked by increased investment in medical technology and a renewed effort to reach out to the community it has served since 1893.

Saint Vincent Hospital's revitalized focus is underscored by its new logo: Its strong but sedate colors are intended to provide a sense of calm and serenity with a contemporary, 21st-century feel. Modern but timeless, the design symbolizes hope and growth with a spiritual undertone — much like the hospital itself. Inspired by the medical center's six-story atrium, the new hospital logo conveys a dual message: Saint Vincent Hospital not only offers community-based and personalized care guided by the spirit of its Catholic roots, it also has expertise and technology on par with its university-based counterparts both locally and in Boston.

Founded by the Sisters of Providence as a small Catholic community-based hospital overlooking the city from Vernon Hill, Saint Vincent Hospital — named for Saint Vincent de Paul — has long been at the forefront of bringing the latest medical and technological advances to patients in Central Massachusetts. During the 1950s, it was one of the first U.S. hospitals outside of a major city to perform open-heart surgery.

Today, Saint Vincent is the only hospital in Central Massachusetts to offer robotically assisted and computer-assisted surgery. Its distinguished team of six specially trained urologic surgeons uses the Da Vinci surgical robot to perform the latest treatment for prostate cancer. Two of the hospital's general surgeons are also trained to use the robotic device for general procedures such as gallbladder and reflux surgery. And the hospital expects to train surgeons to use the Da Vinci for mitral valve repair surgery within the next year. The million-dollar system helps surgeons see vital anatomical features more clearly and perform more precise procedures via a tiny surgical opening. Patients experience less pain, face less risk of infection and recover more quickly.

The hospital's computer-assisted orthopedic surgery — CAOS — offers fresh benefits to patients requiring delicate knee surgery. That system allows surgeons to make bone cuts with unsurpassed precision, which is critical in properly aligning knees. Each surgery is customized to each patient by entering information on their individual anatomy into the system, resulting in a less-invasive procedure with better results for the patient and less recovery time.

Both the Da Vinci and CAOS are part of an array of technology that lets Saint Vincent Hospital's more than 200 credentialed surgeons and other procedurists offer patients the latest techniques in minimally invasive procedures. Besides being only one of three hospitals in the state to have surgeons trained to use the Da Vinci, Saint Vincent Hospital is at the forefront of all types of laparoscopic surgery, notes Dr. Jeffrey Steinberg, FACS, chief of surgery. "In the old days, we only had the option of cutting people

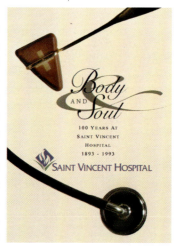

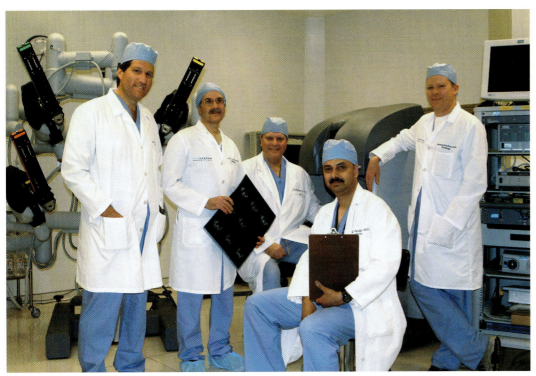

technology may give a more exact picture of the condition." Saint Vincent Hospital is one of only three hospitals in the state to have its echocardiography laboratory nationally accredited.

The division also features the latest technology in ultrasound, called "virtual histology," which allows physicians to pinpoint arterial blockages throughout the body and warn of potential problems in advance, according to Dr. Saperia. This advanced technology is being used by scientific leaders to generate new information about heart disease, he says. The Cardiovascular Division also recently completed a new electrophysiology services lab with state-of-the art computer software allowing physicians to "map" electrical problems of the heart. The lab gives cardiologists the most advanced tools to diagnose and treat electrophysiological heart conditions often associated with the heart beating too fast or too slow.

Yet another key advancement at Saint Vincent Hospital, telemedicine and remote digital programs in its radiology department, lets physicians access results remotely via computer. If, for instance, a patient has a procedure done at the hospital, their doctor in Bangor, Maine, can read the results over the computer.

Saint Vincent Hospital's commitment to provide compassionate and personalized patient care is as strong as its commitment to provide the latest technology. A full-service, 348-bed acute-care hospital, it caters to the needs of all its patients, from newborns to seniors. It has a wide-range of inpatient and outpatient services, including open-heart surgery, radiation, oncology and pediatrics. The hospital also delivers more than 1,700 babies each year. And it does so in a state-of-the art medical center whose amenities — including a six-story atrium with trees and a waterfall, retail shops and restaurants — make it a positive and uplifting presence in the city's downtown. The setting contributes to Saint Vincent Hospital's mission to provide health-care services that emphasize the physical, psychological, social and spiritual well-being of the patients and the community.

"We have tried to maintain that spirit of compassion and family that the hospital was founded to offer," says Dr. George Abraham, the associate program director for the Internal Medicine Residency Program who did his own residency training at Saint Vincent.

At the same time, Dr. Abraham says, Saint Vincent Hospital has the academic credentials and technology that bring physicians from all over the world to train in its graduate medical education program.

Saint Vincent Hospital has a nationally acclaimed Critical Care Center that provides sophisticated care to critically ill or injured patients. Through its collaborative approach, the Critical Care Center, which houses medical, surgical, cardiovascular and coronary ICUs, works to provide the best possible care for each patient.

Continued on next page

ABOVE: SAINT VINCENT HOSPITAL'S DA VINCI ® PROSTATECLONY TEAM (L-R) DR. JEFFREY STEINBERG, CHIEF OF SURGERY; DR. JEFFREY S. ISEN; DR. ROBERT D. BLUTE JR.; DR. BHALCHANDRU PARULKAR; AND DR. SIMON MCRAE

NOT PRESENT WHEN PHOTO WAS TAKEN: DR. WAYNE B. GLAZIER

BELOW: (L-R) MARY ABELLI, FAMILY LIAISON, LYNN HEDMAN, BUSINESS AND INFORMATION SYSTEMS MANAGER; WENDY LANCY, NURSE MANAGER; AND DR. DAVID KAUFMAN, CHIEF OF CRITICAL CARE MEDICINE

open to fix them," he says. "These days we have many minimally invasive procedures."

With "one of the most beautiful and up-to-date hospitals in the country," along with a "superb" nursing staff, supportive administration and reputation for superior patient care, Saint Vincent Hospital attracts the most highly trained surgical staff in Massachusetts, Dr. Jeffrey Steinberg, Chief of Surgery, points out. Graduates from the top surgical training programs — including Harvard, Stanford and The Mayo Clinic — choose to come to Saint Vincent Hospital, says Dr. Steinberg, a Harvard graduate who came to the hospital two years ago as chief of surgery. They bring their expertise to the hospital's surgery divisions: general surgery, vascular surgery, cardiothoracic surgery, otolaryngology, neurosurgery, plastic surgery, ophthalmology, urology and oral surgery.

Another area in which Saint Vincent Hospital has been making technological strides is its Division of Cardiovascular Medicine. The division, which includes 20 physicians, provides patients with all cardiovascular procedures and treatments with the exception of heart transplants. Its non-invasive laboratory features two-dimensional echocardiography, which recently became one of the few systems in the state to become fully digitized, notes Dr. Gordon Saperia, director of the Division of Cardiovascular Medicine. That advancement not only provides more efficient storage and manipulation of diagnostic data but also allows cardiologists to do more sophisticated analysis of cardiovascular conditions, he says. "We may be able to see some things that we couldn't have seen before," says Dr. Saperia. "If someone has a problem with a heart valve, analysis with this

SAINT VINCENT HOSPITAL

Continued from previous page

"We collect a huge amount of data and we review it continuously to determine how to improve our services," says Dr. David Kaufman, chief of Critical Care Medicine.

Here, too, the hospital has broken new ground. While throughout the country, most ICUs are overseen by anesthesiologists or surgeons, Saint Vincent Hospital's ICU is under the direction of an "intensivist," a specialist in the care of the critically ill. Through a collaboration of nurses, doctors and other critical care staff, the Center provides a well-rounded approach to caring for each patient admitted to its care.

In 2001, Saint Vincent Hospital's ICU was singled out as a model of excellence in a report by the Washington, D.C.-based Clinical Advisory Board reviewing ICUs throughout the country in search of ways to elevate the standard of care. The recognition highlighted the effectiveness of Saint Vincent Hospital's Critical Care Center staff's team approach — working together for the good of the patient.

The Hospital's Critical Care team is highly specialized, with nurses trained in critical care working alongside a pharmacist, dietician and respiratory therapist, all specializing in caring for the critically ill patient. Each morning, the team makes rounds together, assuring that team members are on the same page in caring for each individual patient.

In 2002, the National Coalition for Healthcare selected Saint Vincent Hospital's ICU program as one of the 10 best in the country. It was the only hospital in the state to receive this prestigious honor, based on its innovations in the delivery of care as well as its attention to exceptional end-of-life care for patients and their families.

In 2003, the Society of Critical Care Medicine awarded Saint Vincent Hospital it's first-ever Patient and Family Focused ICU Award for exceptional treatment of patients and their families. And in 2005, the Critical Care Center garnered the Department of Health and Human Services' Medal of Honor for setting benchmark standards for organ donations at the hospital — a distinction that it shared with only three other New England hospitals.

Saint Vincent Hospital's Critical Care Center attributes its success to its commitment to working together to put the patient first. The staff works to continually improve its service to the community by analyzing and comparing the extensive ICU data collected to determine how to elevate care

Saint Vincent Hospital has a long tradition as a teaching hospital that dates back to 1899, with its first house officer. Its training program received American Medical Association Council approval in 1914 and gained greater stature with its 1953 affiliation with Georgetown University. Today, Saint Vincent Hospital offers residency programs in cardiology, internal medicine, podiatry and radiology. It also takes part in joint

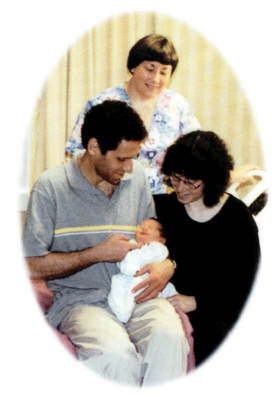

residency programs with the University of Massachusetts Medical School, including cardiothoracic surgery, critical care, emergency medicine, neurology, neurosurgery and Ob/Gyn. The mission of its Department of Medicine and Medicine Residency Program is three-fold: To provide comprehensive and compassionate medical care to its patients; to foster an environment of scholarship and lifelong learning; and to work in a community of colleagues with the highest ethical standards.

"Most people don't know us as a teaching hospital," says Martha Wright, administrator for the Medical Residency Program. "We have been training medical residents for more than 100 years."

Wright notes that Saint Vincent Hospital's teaching programs are so sought after that they get some 2,700 applicants for 32 openings a year. Its osteopathic program is one of only 19 programs nationally which are dually accredited by the American Osteopathic Association and the Accreditation Council for Graduate Medical Education. The residency program offers a collegial atmosphere, where students "can sit and have conversations with the chief physicians," Wright says.

Residents who train at Saint Vincent Hospital go on to prestigious fellowships around the world, though many do return to live and work in the area. Currently, one-third of all graduating medical residents settle in Worcester, showing their dedication to being part of the Saint Vincent Hospital community.

And, Dr. Joel Popkin, director of the Internal Medicine Residency Program, points out, Saint Vincent residents "handsomely win prizes" in state and national poster and abstract competitions before the American College of Physicians. Their work — documenting unique patient cases, research or

ABOVE: SAINT VINCENT HOSPITAL DELIVERED MORE THAN 1,700 BABIES LAST YEAR BELOW: MOTHER MARY OF PROVIDENCE, S.P., FOUNDER AND MOTHER SUPERIOR OF THE SISTERS OF PROVIDENCE

community projects — consistently dominates the top presentations chosen to represent the state in this national medical excellence awards program. In fact, seven of the 10 posters chosen by the American College of Physicians to represent Massachusetts residents and attending physicians in April 2005 were from Saint Vincent Hospital.

Being a teaching hospital, Dr. Joel H. Popkin, Director of Internal Medicine Residency Program, notes, helps Saint Vincent Hospital stay current with the latest in medical and scientific trends and energizes its staff by bringing in residents with a variety of backgrounds and experiences. What Saint Vincent offers students that university-based facilities don't, he says, is a family-like academic atmosphere with a close-knit, one-on-one experience and a chance to interact with the community they serve. "The larger the hospital, the easier one can get lost in it," Dr. Popkin says. At Saint Vincent, the 100 physicians-in-training who enter the residency program have the benefit of working at a closer level with the hospital's entire staff, including its academic faculty. "The quality of the staff and services here are superb," adds Dr. Popkin. "The camaraderie of the people who work here is incredible."

Residents join physicians in making volunteer visits into the community as part of the hospital's continued effort to provide care for the uninsured and the needy, Dr. Abraham points out. "It's all part of the overall spirit of Saint Vincent Hospital," he says.

At the forefront of Saint Vincent Hospital's quest to understand and treat individual patients' needs through personal attention is its 800-member nursing staff. Excellence in nursing is a long tradition at Saint Vincent Hospital and the hospital recognizes that its nurses play a vital role in its ability to deliver quality patient and family-centered care. At the core of that care is the understanding that family members are deeply affected when a family member is ill. The hospital's family-centered approach to patient care embraces spouses, parents, children and significant others as vital participants in the treatment process.

Saint Vincent Hospital offers

ABOVE: (L-R) DR. JANE A. LOCHRIE, ASSOCIATE PROGRAM DIRECTOR, INTERNAL MEDICINE; DR. ANTHONY L. ESPOSITO, CHIEF OF MEDICINE; AND DR. JOEL H. POPKIN, DIRECTOR, INTERNAL MEDICINE RESIDENCY PROGRAM RIGHT: DR. ALLEN W. FILIBERTI CONDUCTING MEDICAL ROUNDS WITH RESIDENTS

professional nurses the opportunity to provide leadership within the health care team. Nurses work collaboratively with physicians and play a critical role, not only in patient care, but in education and research. As well-respected partners in the healing process, Saint Vincent nurses benefit from an environment that fosters self-development and continued learning.

Despite the closing of its nursing education program in 1988, Saint Vincent Hospital takes a leadership role in providing educational opportunities and on-the-job experience for many of the local college nursing programs, including those at Quinsigamond Community College, Becker College and the Massachusetts College of Pharmacy's Accelerated Nursing Program.

The hospital's nursing orientation, called Preceptor, lasts four to eight weeks and includes both generalized and individualized programs based on competency assessments, high practice standards and a desire to promote productivity. Experienced mentoring staff nurses partner with new staff to support and encourage their professional growth.

Saint Vincent Hospital has certainly come a long way from the 12-bed hospital which the Sisters of Providence opened more than a century ago in a drafty farmhouse on Vernon Hill. Not only has it earned a distinguished place among community and teaching hospitals, but it also serves as an economic force in the region it serves. With a workforce of 2,000, it is one of the largest employers in the Greater Worcester area.

The hospital will continue to grow and evolve along with the region and fast-changing medical technology. But its mission will remain the same as it was so many years ago — to deliver quality health care with compassion and integrity. "Our goal is to create opportunity, inspire change and deliver on our promise to provide a quality health care experience in a safe environment, with caregivers dedicated to providing the most passionate and compassionate care to our patients," says John E. Smithhisler, president and CEO of Saint Vincent. "That is what makes Saint Vincent Hospital stand out among health care providers. As we meet the challenges of the future, we will remain committed to the community we have served for more than a century."

ounded in 1896, Perkins in Lancaster is one of the largest human service providers in Central Massachusetts. With 360 employees and operating out of several sites in Lancaster and Clinton, the agency is the second-largest employer in the eight towns served by the Wachusett Chamber of Commerce. The school was originally located in Newton, Mass., and named for Franklin Haskins Perkins, M.D. At that time the school's mission was to serve the mentally retarded but that has changed dramatically. Today the agency provides residential treatment, day education, community behavioral health, community-based living and assisted-living services to a wide variety of children, adolescents, adults and elderly people and their families.

Perkins is a 501(c)(3) not-for-profit organization and relies heavily on philanthropy from individuals, foundations and corporations. In the last 16 years, the school has added eight buildings to its complex largely based on a beautiful hundred-plus-acre main campus on both sides of Main Street in Lancaster. Capital projects, including new construction, program development and innovation, and expansion to new areas of service are heavily dependent on private support.

Currently a regional provider of services, Perkins is quickly moving toward national recognition as a model of service and disseminator of best practices in the fields of child welfare, special education, residential treatment and community-based human services. One hundred ten years of experience and the latest technological advances form the basis for the ongoing search for improved programs and services. The commitment to the agency's motto, "A Chance to Blossom," is stronger than ever.

Twenty-two classrooms ranging from kindergarten through high school encompass the Dr. Franklin Perkins School, which has been called the "premier special education facility in the state." Focusing on the Massachusetts curriculum frameworks, Perkins emphasizes academics with in-depth support services including individual, family and group therapy, speech and language services, Project Read, and technology instruction. Perkins students are prepared for the statewide MCAS exams. The Janeway Education Center, completed in 2002, houses all classes from 6th grade through 12th grade and includes a state-of-the-art library, dining room and auditorium.

Extracurricular activities and after-school programs are comprehensive and serve the varying needs of Perkins students who represent a variety of diagnoses: emotionally disturbed, mentally ill, and

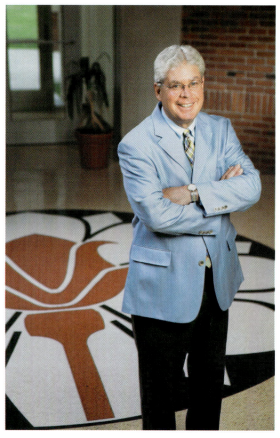

LEFT: CHARLES P. CONROY ED.D,
EXECUTIVE DIRECTOR

behaviorally disordered.

"We're not big on labels" says Executive Director Dr. Charles P. Conroy, "but we are good at assessment and tailor-made programs to meet children's individual needs. Children are placed in the day or residential treatment programs and many have been enrolled at the Perkins School through the state Department of Education and/or Department of

Social Services because of learning difficulties and histories of abuse, neglect or homelessness."

Children and adolescents live on campus or in a community-based group home. The homes are inviting and equipped with the latest in technology. Students are involved in community activities and take part in an extensive social, recreational and leisure activities program. The picturesque campus includes ball fields, bike riding paths, walking trails and a ropes course. Winter months leave children with no fewer options for play and exercise with an indoor pool, gymnasium, teen center, and plenty of space for indoor recreation. Space is shared with local athletic groups and seniors, as well as neighborhood children who enjoy the new playground.

Opened in 2000, Davis Manor is a modern, highly specialized, assisted-living facility located at 200 Harvard Road in Lancaster, which focuses on services to elderly people with developmental disabilities or Alzheimer's Disease. Individualized, quality care for the elderly is the central focus of this service.

Perkins Child and Adolescent Behavioral Health, a community mental health group practice, serves children and families from the surrounding communities. Located at a stand-alone site on Main Street in Lancaster, this department also consults to public school districts in Central Massachusetts concerning in-district programs and services for students with behavioral problems.

Perkins opened a community horsemanship program in 2004 called "Rein in a Dream." Based at its Main Street barn and new indoor riding arena, the program now serves children from all over Worcester County. Many of the children enrolled have special needs that research and experience have shown are ameliorated or remediated through equine-facilitated learning experiences.

Thanks to a donation from a local businessman in 1990, the Barlow Building, a 40,000-square-foot former retail furniture store in Clinton's downtown, was renovated to become a home to 10 Perkins adults with special needs. Also benefiting from the donation are the Clinton senior citizens;

Great Brook Valley Health Center's community dental clinic; and a full-scale training center for Perkins staff, community groups and businesses. Perkins prides itself on developing strong community relationships as evidenced by the sharing of this attractive space.

In the next year construction will start on a new child development center in Lancaster to serve infants, toddlers and preschoolers. It is the result of an assessed need in the area for quality day care and will emphasize services to families in addition to day care for babies and young children.

Perkins is a unique combination of specialized services for children, adults and families in programs that are accredited and licensed by the Joint Commission on the Accreditation of Healthcare Organizations (JCAHO), the Association of Independent Schools in New England and a variety of departments and agencies from all the New England states. The organization's reputation for comprehensive, quality service is unparalleled in the region. Few human-service agencies serve as varied a clientele as Perkins and fewer still do so with as strong an emphasis on quality assurance, program improvement, innovative and entrepreneurial services and family centeredness.

The emphasis on the "human factor" and a strengths-based approach in all Perkins does pervade the large number of programs and services offered to the child, adolescent, adult and elderly.

"It's all meaningless if children and families don't heal and have brighter futures," says Dr. Conroy. "Kids and families need to see tangible evidence of their own progress — but so do all of us who work toward that goal."

LaVIGNE INC.

The presses have been rolling at LaVigne Inc. for more than 100 years. Founded in 1898 by entrepreneur and political enthusiast Narcisse Lavigne, the company has a rich history of leading change and innovation in the print communications industry.

Since its inception, LaVigne has been a Worcester institution. Starting with Narcisse LaVigne's purchase of Kirschner & Sons on Federal Street, the company has been located on Foster Street, Main Street, Mechanic Street, Jackson Street and its current location since 1983 at the Worcester Airport Industrial Park on Coppage Drive.

LaVigne Inc. has always recognized that printing is simply the end process of helping a company establish a strong brand in the marketplace. As early as 1918 Narcisse LaVigne began his company's tradition of strong branding by changing the spelling of his name from Lavigne to LaVigne, noting that the capital 'V' gave the name a more distinctive and sophisticated character. In 1997 the name of the company was changed from LaVigne Press to LaVigne Inc. to reflect the growing number of services the company was providing that were independent from the manufacturing process of printing.

LaVigne takes pride in its Worcester heritage

Narcisse LaVigne died at the young age of 53 in 1930 and was succeeded by his son Robert. In 1968, Robert's son Thomas became president and in 1997 Thomas's son Toby took over the reigns. In 1999, Christopher Wells was elected president of the company, the first non-family leader of the organization, and currently serves in the capacity of president & CEO.

LaVigne Inc. today is a far cry from the traditional vision of a print shop. Since the advent of the Internet as a means of communication, as well as the technological changes that have driven the desktop publishing revolution, LaVigne has transformed into a true marketing communications service provider.

Currently, more than 50% of LaVigne's work comes from corporate Web ordering systems the company hosts. LaVigne has a division devoted to building on-demand communications systems for its

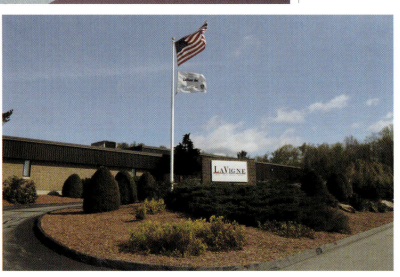

clients that drive print, e-mail, web surveys and other types of communication. The company also fulfills orders for customers in more than 60 countries. High-quality color digital printing (non-existent in 1990) accounts for more than 20% of the company's revenues.

Imagine providing remote sales offices with the ability to customize and order professionally printed materials on-line and have the material delivered anywhere in the world in two days. Imagine transferring handwritten information from a form to an electronic database with no human intervention and generating customized, personalized sales materials based on the relevant data that was captured. These are the types of solutions that are happening today at LaVigne Inc.

LaVigne is recognized as a leader in the print communications business by its peers worldwide. The company's client list reads like a "Who's Who" of Fortune 500 corporations.

Christopher Wells, the current president & CEO, serves on Hewlett Packard's Digital Print Advisory Council (one of only 14 print service providers in North America), The Printing Industry of New England's board of directors, and the Industry Trends Advisory Group. He was also named one of the top 20 visionaries in the industry by *Printing Impressions* magazine.

In keeping with the traditions that have built the company, more than 30% of LaVigne's workforce has been employed by the company for more than 15 years, many for more than 30 years.

Today, LaVigne Inc. prides itself as being one of the top 50 independent commercial printers and one of the top 10 fastest-growing independent commercial printers in the U.S. The company operates 24 hours per day, 6 days per week and services customers all over the world.

LaVigne excels in the ability to consistently deliver a high-quality product within a short period of time while offering exceptional, hands-on service to its clients. LaVigne's commitment to technology is reflected by ongoing recognition by the industry in trade publications and case studies highlighting their innovation and approach to the evolution of print communications.

In fact, LaVigne has been profiled in more than 100 articles and case studies worldwide. LaVigne received international recognition in July, 2005, by winning the CIP4 International Print Production Innovation Award for Biggest Improvement in Efficiency and Customer Responsiveness as a Result of Process Automation by the CIP4 Organization in Zurich, Switzerland. LaVigne was the only U.S. based company to receive mention.

LaVigne Inc.'s core competencies are in 2-8+ color conventional offset runs of 5,000 to 200,000+; shorter run, quick turn, 4-6 color digital printing that rivals offset for quality; On Demand Communications systems including Web-to-print, trigger and event-based variable data solutions, fulfillment on demand, data acquisition and management; training; mailing; kitting; and fulfillment.

Worcester Envelope Company is the largest regional independent manufacturer in the Northeast, providing an exceptional onsite management team that provides the necessary support for quick response for day-to-day operations. As a family owned and operated business, the company has been committed to providing the best service to the community for more than 100 years.

Worcester Envelope Company began operations in 1893 in the heart of the city of Worcester. From that beginning, the company has grown to become a world-class leader as a provider of quality envelopes, mailing resources and packaging.

Their main focus has always been the high-speed production of the industry's best quality envelopes. However, through recent endeavors, they are now capable of offering complete mailing and packaging solutions for paper-based communication.

With an eye toward the future, the Worcester Envelope Company will continue to provide the highest-quality envelope products while investing energy into expanding operations in order to bring a wider array of products and services to the business community they serve.

By manufacturing quality products and using the most advanced equipment and technology, Worcester Envelope Company offers products to many industries, including: insurance, financial, banking, government, publishing, medical and retail.

On July 24, 1893, Worcester Envelope Company was incorporated for the "purpose of manufacturing and selling paper goods, stationery and paper-handling machinery." The president from 1893 to 1898 was Henry S. Pratt. Ezra Waterhouse was one of the original stockholders and was elected president in 1898 and continued in that office until 1928. Some of the early envelope machines designed and built in the United States were the work of Ezra Waterhouse.

In 1929, the news of the stock market crash sent panic throughout the industrial sector. Worcester Envelope carried on its business sensibly. By 1933, the country's banking system collapsed and the country was in the midst of the Depression. George Grant became president of the company and carried it through those worrisome times. On September 2, 1952, Grant retired after 50 years of continuous service.

Worcester Envelope Company was established on Foster Street in Worcester in the area now occupied by the new Medical City and was our home

for 85 years (1893-1978). Experiencing a period of rapid growth, the company found it necessary to build a new facility in Auburn and, in 1978, moved to its present location. During 1980s, the company continued its growth in the industry. In 1987, Eldon Pond III joined the company and became president in 1997.

Throughout its rich history, Worcester Envelope Company has changed with the times, offering state-of-the-art techniques and services as well as continuing its commitment to quality customer service.

Critical business needs demand that the company focus its efforts on providing consistent high-quality products with cost-effective systems and reliable, on-time deliveries. The foundation of Worcester Envelope Company's success is the commitment of everyone in sales, customer service, scheduling, production, accounting, shipping, and management to satisfy precise business needs for each customer. Worcester Envelope builds long-standing relationships by combining the hard work of its dedicated employees with the most advanced technology available.

WORCESTER ENVLOPE HAS KEPT PACE WITH THE LATEST TECHNOLOGY WITHOUT COMPROMISING OUR QUALITY STANDARDS

SAINT FRANCIS HOME

The history of Saint Francis Home is inextricably intertwined with that of the Little Franciscans of Mary, who founded the Home in 1889 as an act of love and mercy. Originally, they opened the Home for orphans on Southgate Street near Saint Ann's Chapel in Worcester. Within two years, the Home sheltered 250 children and 15 aged and infirm.

In October 1891, the Sisters relocated to a two-story frame building on Bleeker Street in the Grafton Hill section of the city. The Sisters begged for alms to care for their charges and endured many hardships.

In January 1898, the Sisters devoted themselves exclusively to the care of the elderly because of the increasing need. So many men and women sought admission to Saint Francis Home that a new four-story brick edifice was built in 1908 on Thorne Street, boasting the marvel of an elevator.

Subsequent years brought many changes and modernizations. In 1983, the Little Franciscans of Mary surrendered control and the future direction of the Home to a lay board of directors who remain committed to the original mission to serve all people regardless of their race, religion, national origin or economic circumstance. With the advent of another addition in 1984, the address became 101 Plantation St.

In July 1990, the facility was certified to accept 100 Medicare-eligible residents. This number was increased to 137 in September 1993, which is the current capacity. The strong reputation of the Home continues today.

To carry on this tradition, the Board of Directors has embarked on an ambitious plan to relocate the Home to 101 Barry Road, Worcester. A state-of-the-art long-term care facility will be constructed at the site of Our Lady of Mercy Health Care, a rest home for the Sisters of Mercy.

Collaborating partners are Saint Francis Community Health Care Inc., the Sisters of the Presentation, Religious Venerini Sisters, Sisters of the Assumption and the Sisters of Mercy, who own the land. Together, they are creating the new Saint Francis Home at Mercy, which will be built in 2006.

The design of the residents' rooms is unique, allowing each person a view of the beautiful grounds, more private space and comfortable furnishings. The physical surroundings in the new facility will match the excellent clinical care that now exists.

In addition, the Home will feature a contemporary chapel, private dining rooms, exceptional therapy space and a Gerontology Center. Utilizing the expertise of the Home's staff and partnering with nearby colleges, agencies and healthcare systems, the Center will explore the many facets of aging and related issues. The Center will be a forum for the public to reflect on the many changes that occur in senior years. It will be a dynamic environment for learning.

The demand for quality long-term care and respect for life is growing. The new Saint Francis Home at Mercy will meet the community's needs well into the 21st century.

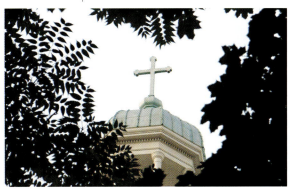

ASSUMPTION COLLEGE

Assumption College has been consistently ranked among the top-tier colleges in the Northeast—and for good reason. Once a small, Catholic, liberal arts college geared toward serving the needs of the area's Franco-Americans in the early 1900s, Assumption has prospered and grown in the last century to become Worcester's largest campus, with more than 175 park-like acres and a physical plant designed to meet the growing technological needs of today's students.

Diverse and enriching academic programs are offered at the under-graduate, graduate and continuing education levels by dedicated faculty, many of whom are well published in their fields, but remain committed to teaching. For example, Assumption offers one of the most comprehensive Business Studies program in the region, from certificate programs to associate's, bachelor's and master's degree programs. Undergraduate science majors are studying in the state-of-the-art Testa Science Center on campus. Some students are engaged in research opportunities with faculty, while others work off-campus with renowned scientists in Worcester's medical research community.

Undergraduate Education and graduate Special Education students are excelling in the classroom as student teachers in local and regional elementary and secondary schools. Psychology students have an opportunity to learn from faculty members who have developmental and clinical backgrounds. Social and Rehabilitation Counseling students intern with regional agencies and organizations, gaining insights into how a diverse community requires a unique support system.

These represent just a sampling of the more than 75 academic programs offered at the college, complemented by a growing number of credit and non-credit on-line courses. Experiential learning at both the undergraduate and graduate levels, such as internships, practicums, student teaching, Community Service Learning and study abroad provide additional opportunities to develop critical thinking skills.

Co-curricular opportunities for undergraduates enhance the learning experience at this primarily residential college, where more than 90% of undergrad-

ABOVE: THE RICHARD AND JANET TESTA SCIENCE CENTER TAKES CENTER STAGE ON ASSUMPTION'S SALISBURY STREET CAMPUS

LEFT: ITS ATRIUM IS OFTEN USED FOR EVENTS SUCH AS SHAKESPEARE'S *ROMEO AND JULIET*

ABOVE: THE "HOUNDS"
BASKETBALL PEP RALLY
RIGHT: ASSUMPTION
STUDENTS HAVE MANY
OPPORTUNITIES TO ENHANCE
THEIR EDUCATION OUTSIDE THE
CLASSROOM, SUCH AS HAVING
AN INTERNSHIP AS A
LEGISLATIVE ASSISTANT AT
WORCESTER'S SMALL
BUSINESS SERVICE BUREAU
(SBSB)

uate students reside on campus all four years. More than 400 students are engaged in the Northeast 10, Division II athletics program, where Assumption constantly rates among the top nationally for its high graduation rate among its athletes.

Assumption College is also actively engaged in community affairs, with more than one third of its undergraduate students serving as community volunteers with the Worcester Public Schools and local social service agencies. The college is host to the very successful Worcester Institute for Senior Education (W.I.S.E.), a member-run, Learning-in-Retirement program open to senior citizens in Central Massachusetts. Community engagement is also enhanced by the college's Ecumenical Institute, French Institute, Beck Institute and National Catholic Center for Student Aspirations (NCCSA), as well as by cultural opportunities created by the College's HUMANARTS program and its d'Alzon Arts Series.

MISSION:

Assumption College, rooted in the Catholic intellectual tradition, strives to form graduates known for critical intelligence, thoughtful citizenship and compassionate service. We pursue these ambitious goals through a curriculum grounded in the liberal arts and extending to the domain of professional studies. Enlivened by the Catholic affirmation of the harmony of faith and reason, we aim, by the pursuit of the truth, to transform the minds and hearts of students. Assumption favors diversity and ecumenically welcomes all who share its goals.

As it celebrates its 90th anniversary, the law firm of Mirick O'Connell carries on the tradition of its founders, yet has grown with the times to meet today's complex needs.

Mirick O'Connell's roots run strong in Massachusetts. The firm was founded by Worcester native George Hammond Mirick, a Harvard Law School graduate who began practicing law in 1909 and started his own firm in Worcester in 1916. Mirick concentrated on real estate, corporate and estate law — practice areas that are still important to the firm today. He was joined by Paul Revere O'Connell in 1930, Gardener G. DeMallie in 1936, and Lawrence H. Lougee in 1955.

Over the past 30 years, the firm has more than quadrupled in size, and earned a reputation as a comprehensive business law firm. The firm has also expanded beyond Worcester, adding offices in Westboro and Boston to better serve our clients throughout the region. Our attorneys appear before state and federal courts and administrative bodies across the country.

Mirick O'Connell is committed to community service. Among the firm's attorneys are officers, trustees and directors of civic and charitable organizations, coaches, scoutmasters and members of many educational and cultural groups. The firm has sponsored many charitable endeavors and has donated legal services to many non-profit organizations. Our attorneys have held significant leadership positions in many revitalization and redevelopment efforts throughout Worcester County. Mirick O'Connell is also a leader in the legal community. Our attorneys have served as presidents and officers of the Worcester County Bar Association and the Massachusetts Bar Association, and have held leadership positions in many other legal organizations.

Today, as Mirick O'Connell marks its 90th anniversary of service, we combine talent, leadership and a wealth of experience to provide exceptional service to clients

ABOVE: (L-R) THE MIRICK O'CONNELL MANAGEMENT COMMITTEE, ATTORNEYS PAUL J. D'ONFRO, DAVID E. SURPRENANT, JOSEPH M. HAMILTON AND PETER J. DAWSON

throughout New England and across the world.

Mirick O'Connell takes pride in our versatility. We are a full-service firm that is large enough to provide the depth of services needed in today's complex legal environment, yet focused on delivering personal attention to each client and matter. Whether serving large corporate clients, entrepreneurs, research pioneers, public or private school systems or an individual, the firm's client focus is central to our philosophy.

We see the attorney-client relationship as the foundation of strong and effective legal representation. Each client works with an attorney who serves as a client manager, maintaining open lines of communication and updating the client on issues of importance. We take the time to learn about our clients to better enable us to address their immediate needs and help them develop long-term plans. Our unique continuity of representation has proven to be an efficient and effective way to provide quality, personalized legal representation to our clients.

Uncompromising service has been the embodiment of Mirick O'Connell since George Hammond Mirick first opened the doors 90 years ago. Building on our traditional strengths, Mirick O'Connell has embraced new and evolving areas of the law in our continuing commitment to provide the finest service to our clients and the community. As the firm heads into our second century, we are guided by the principles established by our founders: dedication to service, trust, good judg-

ment, and intelligence make Mirick O'Connell a true leader among law firms.

THE KATZ COMPANIES

The Katz Companies represents excellence. Since 1915, the real estate firm founded by Lewis Katz in Worcester, has specialized in meeting the needs of businesses and industries within the I-495/Central Massachusetts corridor and now serves Connecticut and the United Kingdom.

The strong manufacturing base of metropolitan Worcester was the driving force behind the firm's founding 90 years ago.

Lewis Katz believed then that if a brokerage firm could be established, which would provide customers and clients with an unmatched depth of knowledge and understanding of the commercial and industrial market, a successful, profitable relationship could be forged.

His grandson, Myron Lewis Katz, was the primary reason for the family's business success since the 1950s, with his legendary leadership, wisdom, depth of knowledge and vision. "Myron is clearly the most widely respected real estate executive in Central Massachusetts," comments his brother, Howard Katz, now The Katz Companies CEO.

"Over the years we've seen real estate cycles come and go. Today, our clients benefit not only from our years of experience, but also from our creativity and high standards of excellence," Katz says.

Nothing travels faster than the word of a satisfied customer, and from the beginning The Katz Companies has experienced a large volume of repeat business.

The firm's client base ranges from young, rapidly growing companies to regional, national and multi-national corporations. The numbers speak for themselves. The Katz Companies are currently responsible for the listing of more than 60 industrial and office properties, for a total of several million square feet. The firm covers Central Massachusetts, Connecticut and now has a special United Kingdom link, covering space requirements for businesses looking for space throughout Britain.

The firm's long list of customers and clients includes such industry leaders as Quaker Oats, AngusPrime, Devens Commerce Center, DB Riley, Protocol Telecommunications, Woodmeister, WXLO, WPI, UMass Memorial, Parker International Corporation, Weetabix, IDX, Protector Group, Marriott International, Massachusetts College of Pharmacy and Allied Sciences, and a host of others.

Central Massachusetts, Connecticut and the United Kingdom may have been known for manufacturing in the past, but more and more they are

evolving into upscale, metropolitan environments. With all their assets and amenities, the regions are becoming a natural choice for a number of businesses seeking a convenient location.

And with its specialized site search process, The Katz Companies is the firm of choice for companies looking to establish a presence or expand in Central Massachusetts, Connecticut and Great Britain.

The firm's research department prepares an extensive, detailed proposal for each client, analyzing the pros and cons of a number of properties before making a recommendation on a particular site.

With such intense preparation, the company remains committed to its mission of exceeding the expectations of its clients and helping the region to flourish positively.

"There is a certain amount of skill involved in making a match between a building and a client," says Katz. "We see ourselves as the front-line business people linking business, science and industry with the best properties."

Now in its tenth decade, The Katz Companies is expanding for an even brighter future.

And from one generation to the next, excellence, experience and innovation have positioned The Katz Companies to meet the challenges of the future in partnership with the region.

ABOVE: (L-R) DAVID BURWICK,
ANDREW E. MURRAY JR.,
DANIEL BILZ, CARL BURWICK,
HOWARD KATZ, JOHN SCANLON,
BIJAN AZARBYJANI AND MYRON KATZ

FUSARO, ALTOMARE & ERMILIO

Entrepreneurial spirit and a proud tradition unite to make Fusaro, Altomare & Ermilio one of Central Massachusetts' leading law firms; a firm that is dedicated to building enduring and respectful relationships with clients and the community.

Fusaro, Altomare & Ermilio (FA&E) is a prominent Worcester law firm with a history that dates back to 1917. FA&E was founded with a mission: "Respect clients and build their trust." The mission holds true today and has evolved to include a focus on dynamic management. Attorney and Managing Partner John N. Altomare feels that being dynamic ensures that the firm is ever-poised to respond to the changing needs of its business and individual clients.

Client needs have changed dramatically through the years. As a result they demand a higher level of professional expertise and representation from their law firms. In response, FA&E has developed specialty practice areas to better serve its clients. They include corporate and business planning, estate, business and tax planning, estate and trust administration, asset protection, litigation, commercial and residential real estate, and domestic and family law.

The practice areas are staffed by professionals dedicated to finding innovative solutions to each client's personal or business challenges. FA&E attorneys are tenacious advocates who take special pride in standing with their clients every step of the way. Their services range from managing legal complexities and regulatory issues, protecting and preserving wealth and assets, to helping clients expand their personal and business opportunities.

FA&E serves both individual and business clients, with business clients ranging from sole proprietorships up to companies with more than 100 employees. Industries represented include manufacturing, medical, product distribution, business services, technology, non-profits and real estate. While the majority of clients are based in Central Massachusetts, the firm represents clients across the United States, many of whom conduct business globally.

Over the last century, FA&E has also been committed to community service. Contributions include the commissioning of the Christopher Columbus statue that stands in Washington Square today, funding for the chapel at Venerini Academy in Worcester and for building classrooms at Boston

University School of Law. A major sponsor of the Injury Prevention Classic golf tournament, they also support the neonatology unit at UMass Memorial Medical Center. FA&E is a supporting sponsor for the International Charitable Foundation golf tournament. Community service is encouraged and every attorney is involved.

FA&E has been a steadfast believer in Worcester and expects that the city will experience significant business growth and development into the future. In response, the firm took additional space at its downtown headquarters in 2004, more than doubling its existing space. FA&E has grown from five to 12 attorneys and employs a total of 23 people. Attorney Altomare projects that by 2006 the firm will increase staff to include 15 attorneys and will push eastward.

"Our plans are to continue to provide the same level of excellence at Central Massachusetts rates," he says. "We will also maintain our roots in Central Massachusetts."

Internally, FA&E strives to balance the profit goal with a positive work environment. Respect for staff's free time, for their personal and family needs, and for their ideas are key. "If people are happy at work," Altomare says, "they will treat their clients the same way."

ABOVE: DELIVERING INNOVATIVE SOLUTIONS IN AN EVER-CHANGING LEGAL ENVIRONMENT IS KEY FOR ATTORNEYS (L-R) MARK LEE, JOHN ALTOMARE, THOMAS SCANNELL, STEVEN MURPHY, BRENDAN KING AND OTHER MEMBERS OF THE FA&E TEAM BELOW: "OUR ATTORNEYS ARE TENACIOUS ADVOCATES WHO TAKE SPECIAL PRIDE IN STANDING BY THEIR CLIENTS EVERY STEP OF THE WAY." – ATTORNEY JOHN N. ALTOMARE, MANAGING PARTNER

GREENBERG, ROSENBLATT, KULL AND BITSOLI, P.C.

reenberg, Rosenblatt, Kull & Bitsoli, P.C. (GRKB) offers a full range of accounting, income tax, estate and financial planning, business valuation and management advisory services to businesses and individuals.

The firm's roots in downtown Worcester date back to 1921, when Hyman Brodsky opened an office of public accounting on Main Street. In 1956, Nathan Greenberg joined him, co-founding the entity now known as GRKB.

From its beginning as a small local practice, GRKB has expanded to become a full-service public accounting firm with a dedicated staff of more than 50 individuals serving closely held and publicly owned businesses, not-for-profit organizations and individuals.

Attentiveness to client service embodies our firm's management philosophy. We understand that the success of our firm depends on our ability to consistently provide high-quality, proactive and responsive service to our clients, and our professionals are honored to be considered trusted business advisors. To that end, we are committed to working closely with our clients and their other business advisors to gain an understanding of their particular business processes and personal philosophies so that we can assist in designing creative solutions relating to specific opportunities or challenges.

We at GRKB recognize that the quality of the service we provide is a direct result of the knowledge and dedication of our professional staff. Our talented staff possesses the practical knowledge and extensive capabilities that come with years of serving a variety of organizations. Further, each professional keeps their technical skills current and expands their level of expertise through continuing education and professional training.

GRKB has a diverse client base, ranging from individual proprietors to multi-national corporations representing a broad spectrum of industries including: manufacturing, health care, leasing, retail, distribution, advertising, education, construction, automobile dealerships, investment funds, biotechnology, professional service organizations, employee benefit plans and real estate operations (including HUD).

Our audit, review and compilation services provide management, investors, lenders and other third parties the required level of confidence in the financial information they rely on to make business and investment decisions. As part of our commitment to maintaining and improving the quality of our audit and accounting services, we belong to the

American Institute of Certified Public Accountants (AICPA) and are a member of selected practice sections. We also participate in a rigorous quality control process and have consistently been found to comply with the standards set by the AICPA.

In addition to the preparation of a wide variety of tax returns, we perform a multiplicity of federal, state and local tax services for clients including: tax planning and forecasting, tax controversy representation, and developing and evaluating strategies dealing with employee benefits, executive compensation, payment of dividends and distributions, and tax-effective corporate reorganizations (including mergers and acquisitions).

Management advisory and financial consulting services augment the accounting and tax services offered by GRKB. We have a long history of helping our clients increase their profits by assisting them in strengthening internal controls, identifying financial and non-financial performance metrics, reviewing and revising inventory costing techniques, developing budgets, and identifying sources of funding. We also have extensive experience in matters concerning corporate governance and management succession planning.

GRKB's certified valuation analysts (CVAs) are available to conduct business valuations needed for a variety of purposes, including buy-sell agreements, estate planning and gifting, mergers and acquisitions, and divorce. These formal valuations can reduce the risk of subsequent disputes or legal challenges and help avoid personal or emotional biases that may inappropriately influence decisions. Additionally, members of our professional staff have served as expert witnesses in matters involving business valuations.

Wealth creation and asset preservation are two important objectives of our individual clients. We are able to facilitate their fulfillment of these aspirations by offering significant expertise in the areas of financial, retirement and estate planning. GRKB's experienced professionals assist individuals and families in defining their financial, family and philanthropic desires and articulating them in the form of attainable goals. Working in conjunction with other professionals (including attorneys, investment advisors and insurance agents), we help ensure that personal financial plans, trust documents, gifting strategies and wills are consistent with the pre-established goals.

GRKB is a member of JHI, an international association of independent business advisors with more than 150 member firms in more than 55 countries. Through our affiliation with JHI, our clients have access to top-quality professional support wherever their business takes them.

At GRKB, concerned citizenship is more than just a high ideal — it is a working principle. Employees are encouraged to get involved in their profession and their communities. Many of our energetic and dedicated employees volunteer their time and talents to a wide variety of civic, economic and charitable activities, as well as to professional organizations including the Federal Tax Division of the AICPA, the Board of Directors and various committees of the Massachusetts Society of CPAs, the Massachusetts Board of Public Accountancy, and the Better Business Bureau of Central New England.

Building on its traditional strengths, GRKB is dedicated to providing outstanding tax and accounting services to clients in and around the Worcester area in the years to come.

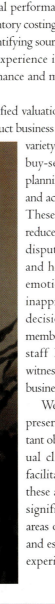

RIGHT: RICHARD F. POWELL, CPA, SENIOR VICE PRESIDENT

BELOW: DIANE L. LECLAIR, CPA, MBA, SENIOR VICE PRESIDENT

WRIGHT LINE LLC

Of or nearly 75 years Wright Line has pioneered solutions to meet the specific requirements of evolving technologies in the workplace. From its modest beginnings as a manufacturer of tabulating card files and accessories to its current operations as a premier manufacturer of consoles, enclosures, office and other specialty furniture for technology-intensive environments, Wright Line has made its mark on many of today's leading corporations.

Founded in 1934 by E. Stanley Wright, the company's early days were dedicated to the design, manufacture and marketing of specialized filing and referencing systems for early data processing environments. Through the 1940s — despite a world war and fluctuating steel prices and availability — the company continued to grow. As the growth and use of computers created an explosion in the methods of maintaining and processing business information, Wright Line expanded its product development initiatives — remaining a leader in the field of business records management.

Gold Star operations

In 1956, Wright Line consolidated all of its operations in its current headquarters at 160 Gold Star Blvd. in Worcester. For the first time the entire operation resided under one roof, improving communication between manufacturing and administration.

Over the years, the company name has changed — from Barry Wright Corporation to APW Wright Line and most recently back to the original Wright Line — and satellite sites have come and gone in response to marketplace fluctuations and product demand. However, the Gold Star plant and the work ethic of the individuals who work within it remain the cornerstone of Wright Line as much today as they did when E. Stanley Wright opened the doors.

Today, the headquarters operation contains Wright Line's administrative offices, sales management, marketing, research and engineering, customer service and manufacturing operations in a 238,000-square-foot facility. The company has established a state-of-the-art, flexible cellular product flow facility, which allows the company to easily adapt to changing capacity and product performance.

In 1995, the company installed a state-of-the-art

robotic powder coat paint line that streamlines the finishing process and gives Wright Line products a finish that is 10 times more durable than traditional finishes. And, the system is environmentally sound, virtually eliminating waste and chemical exposure. Additionally, since 1998, the company has invested some $13 million in manufacturing equipment to

ABOVE: WRIGHT LINE'S CORPORATE HEADQUARTERS ON GOLD STAR BOULEVARD — HOME TO ONE OF NEW ENGLAND'S LARGEST FABRICATORS OF COLD-ROLLED STEEL

LEFT: WRIGHT LINE'S PROFILE COMMUNICATION CONSOLES, ERGONOMIC, HEIGHT-ADJUSTABLE WORKSTATIONS FOR 9-1-1 CALL-TAKERS AND DISPATCHERS, ARE WIDELY USED IN LAW ENFORCEMENT AGENCIES THROUGHOUT THE COUNTRY

enhance production efficiencies and position it for future growth and success.

Product development

In 1964, Wright Line gained worldwide recognition with the invention of the TapeSeal Belt, a product that revolutionized the storage of magnetic computer tape. Then in 1972, the company introduced its Optimedia Storage System, a complete line of modular multimedia storage cabinets that could be reconfigured to meet the demands of advancing technology and changing work environments. Unlike traditional filing cabinets that address limited filing formats, Optimedia allows you to store everything from conventional documentation and hanging files to advanced multimedia storage including DVDs, CDs, 4mm and 8mm tapes, data cartridges and more.

From there the company had a series of successful product introductions — from the first dedicated computer stand to its modular office product line, LINX, one of its largest and longest-running lines that enjoys considerable sales still today.

In 1993, LMS (LAN Management System) stormed the market. This modular, open-architecture furniture system was originally designed for local area networks and communications support applications. In slightly more than four years the company had realized some 50,000 installations throughout the world. And, along with LINX, the LMS product line remains one of the company's most popular to date. Today, its use has expanded into electronic and software labs, video editing suites and many other technology environments.

Within the last decade, the transition to server enclosures — also commonly know as racks — was taking place in the data center. Wright Line was at the forefront of that market with the introduction of LAN Locker MVP, a multi-vendor compatible enclosure system for the freestanding computer servers that were storing and processing business-critical information within virtually every company in the world. It did not matter what server platform — or mix of platforms — that a company was standardized on. This multi-vendor compatible enclosure — or rack — could effectively house any server on the market. There was no need to purchase proprietary racks from the server manufacturer, thus increasing flexibility for the data center manager — another boon for this Worcester-based business.

As the computer industry moved toward rack-mount servers, Wright Line evolved with it. And, as the form-factors of servers continue to shrink — to blades, for instance — Wright Line continues to address those needs with its varied enclosure offering. The genesis of its enclosure line, LAN Locker MVP, has since evolved into more current enclosure offerings that can effectively store, cool, power, manage and secure up to 12kW of equipment in one enclosure. Corporate data centers represent a very large part of where Wright Line does business today. From server farms to Network Operations Centers (NOCs), the company's enclosures, consoles and other products furnish IT environments in some of today's most notable corporations.

A key aspect of Wright Line's profitability is its highly responsive, closed-loop feedback system between its direct sales force and its marketing, engineering and product development teams. Wright Line's flexible manufacturing model allows the engineering and development teams to respond to market requests for add-on features — or even requests for complete product redesigns — in a matter of weeks rather than months. The ability to provide customers with rapid solutions and customized products distinguishes Wright Line from its competitors and allows the company to quickly respond to market shifts or enter new markets quickly. For instance, in June 2002, Wright Line identified the opportunity to develop an innovative desk solution for the public safety/dispatch communication market. In just three years, Wright Line has stormed the market with its Profile Communication Console, which now represents a rapidly growing percentage of its sales.

Wright Line today

Wright Line continues its leadership position as a quality manufacturer of premier console, enclosure, office and other specialty furniture solutions for technology-intensive environments. Whether it's a research and development laboratory at a notable Fortune 500 company, a corporate data center at a leading financial services organization, a large emergency dispatch center in a major metropolitan city or a computer training lab at a local college or university, Wright Line offers a full range of product solutions for any technology-based environment.

FALLON CLINIC

allon Clinic is a multi-specialty medical group with more than 240 primary care doctors and specialists practicing throughout Central Massachusetts. It is also one of the most dynamic and progressive health care organizations in the country.

Fallon Clinic's ability to forge this national reputation is directly attributable to the superior quality of its team of physicians across a broad spectrum of specialties. These 240 highly skilled and trained physicians are supported by 1,700 employees, all using state-of-the-art technology to deliver care in nearly 30 locations. In all, Fallon Clinic provides comprehensive care for more than 1 million patient visits a year.

For more than 75 years, Fallon Clinic has been synonymous with innovation, leadership and health care quality, and continues to challenge convention and transform patient care paradigms. Fallon Clinic has now embarked on a mission to extend its reputation for quality care, and is establishing a new "gold standard" in service excellence in health care delivery.

Fallon Clinic is making significant investments in its clinical facilities, technology and equipment, ensuring that its physicians work in a sophisticated environment that facilitates and enhances their practice of medicine, thus enabling them to deliver an unmatched level of service to patients. Some of these advancements include the use of hospital-based robotic and minimally invasive surgical operations, nuclear cardiology and videostroboscopy, as well as numerous successful disease management programs and multidisciplinary programs addressing infertility, incontinence and obesity, to name a few. Fallon Clinic physicians have admitting privileges at all of the hospitals within its service area, including Worcester Medical Center, where many of its specialty services are based.

Fallon Clinic is also at the forefront of medical and information technology, adding an Electronic Health Record system and digital radiology. These investments encompass computerized medical records for online prescription information, test results, clinical notes and other clinical processes, resulting in a higher level of patient safety. In the back-office, Fallon Clinic has invested in automation systems to simplify the operation of its practice to provide greater efficiency and productivity — from appointments and scheduling to billing.

Fallon Clinic physicians have also greatly expanded access to their care by now accepting all health insurances, such as Aetna, Blue Cross Blue Shield of Massachusetts, Fallon Community Health Plan,

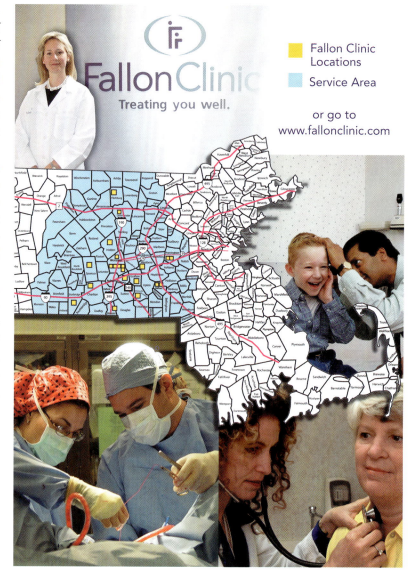

Harvard Pilgrim Health Care, Tufts Health Plan, United Healthcare and others. This enables access to care for nearly 100% of Massachusetts residents with health insurance benefits.

Ultimately, our focus is on our patients. By employing high-caliber physicians and staff, and providing them with innovative technologies, equipment and facilities, patients at Fallon Clinic benefit from the vast resources of compassion and experience ready to serve their health care needs in an atmosphere that is both professional and comfortable.

FALLON CLINIC OFFERS A WIDE RANGE OF PRIMARY CARE, MEDICAL AND SURGICAL SPECIALTY SERVICES ACROSS CENTRAL MASSACHUSETTS AND IN THE METROWEST AREA

ANNA MARIA COLLEGE

or the past six decades, Anna Maria College has provided students with a career-oriented, liberal arts education based on Catholic teaching.

Founded in 1946 by the Sisters of Saint Anne, the college was originally located at a temporary campus at Saint Anne's Academy in Marlboro, Mass. It was moved to its present 190-acre site in Paxton, Mass., in 1952.

Since its founding, the college has provided a quality education to its students while fostering intellectual curiosity, religious sensitivity and social awareness.

Anna Maria College offers bachelor of arts, bachelor of science and bachelor of music degrees with more than 25 areas of concentration. The college offers master's degrees in Counseling Psychology, Fire Science and Administration, Pastoral Ministry, Visual Arts, Business Administration, Education, Criminal Justice, Emergency Management, and Occupational and Environmental Health and Safety, as well as an interdisciplinary certificate of advanced graduate studies. In addition, Anna Maria offers an associate's degree in Business Administration as well as a certificate in Paralegal Studies.

In response to the severe statewide nursing shortage and federal projections that show Massachusetts could face a shortage of more than 9,000 nurses by 2010 and a shortage of more than 25,000 nurses by 2020, the college is developing an associate's degree in nursing. Graduates of the two-year program, which includes summers, will be qualified to become registered nurses upon passing the national NCLEX examination. This new program will add to the college's existing registered nurse/Bachelor of Science degree in nursing, as well as its special programs in school nursing, parish nursing and gerontology nursing.

"The demand for nurses continues to far exceed the supply, and some experts predict that the U.S. will need 1 million new nurses by 2010," says William D. McGarry, president of the college. "Aging baby boomers require more medical care and the current nursing workforce is approaching retirement age." Since 1981, 200 nurses have graduated from the bachelor nursing program. The college expects this number to increase as the program continues to grow.

Due to Anna Maria's tradition of commitment to social awareness and community involvement, the college also established The Molly Bish Center for the Protection of Children and the Elderly in

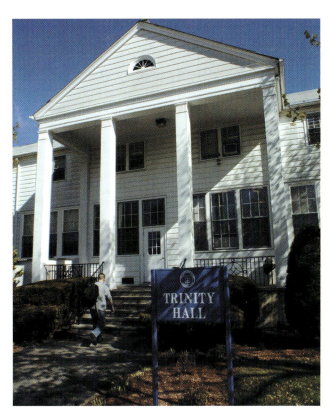

April, 2004. The center is named for 16-year-old Molly Bish, a lifeguard who disappeared from her post at Comins Pond in Warren, Mass., in June, 2000. Molly's remains were found three years later less than five miles from her home.

The Center offers seminars to train, educate and conduct research that will prepare law enforcement personnel, educators, social workers, others in public service and members of the community at large to prevent and respond to crimes against children and the elderly.

A network of nature trails winds through Anna Maria's 190-acre campus, offering opportunities for solitude, contemplation and experiential learning for environmental science, ecology and biology majors. The trails are open to students and the public and include a forest, meadow, wetlands, streams and a pond.

SEVEN HILLS FOUNDATION

even Hills Foundation's roots reach back as far as 1951, when a group of families had a dream to find support and educational programs for their loved ones who lived each and every day with a disability. From that small but very ambitious beginning was born what is today one of the largest human service organizations in the Commonwealth of Massachusetts.

Based in Worcester, Seven Hills Foundation and its health and human service affiliates reach every region of the state through its network of more than 130 clinical sites and residences. Seven Hills Foundation offers an array of health services and clinical supports to children and adults challenged by emotional, behavioral, cognitive, physical or developmental disabilities. The mission of Seven Hills Foundation continues to be *"... to promote and encourage the empowerment of people with significant challenges so that each may pursue their highest possible degree of personal well-being and independence."*

Seven Hills Foundation supports children, adults and seniors through a continuum of community-based services, including residential and respite care options; school supports and consultation; pediatric care for medically fragile children; behavioral health counseling and treatment; supported employment and related adult day services; therapeutic recreation; and other services intended to enhance the health and welfare of Massachusetts citizens.

Working together with our many friends in the Greater Worcester area, we are building a brighter future that will ensure that the disabled and those facing life challenges in our communities will be able to live a life of fulfillment, will experience all that is great about being part of a larger and loving community, and will continue to dream bigger than they dared to just a few years ago.

Not unlike the many individuals who participate in our programs, we at Seven Hills Foundation set goals — goals for the work we will undertake on behalf of these very individuals. The goals we set each year are thought to be too ambitious by some, but we know that with our outstanding partners in the Greater Worcester area, we can set and achieve almost anything — nothing is beyond our reach.

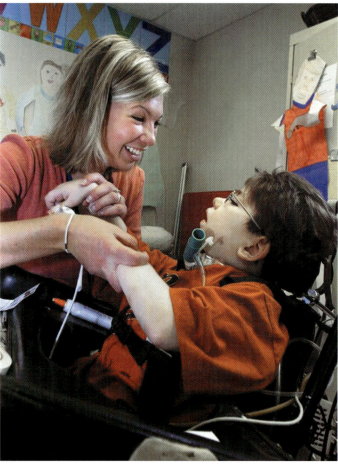

Seven Hills Foundation is fortunate to have forged such strong partnerships within the Worcester area. Charitable organizations, businesses and individuals, all of whom work with us each year, contribute significantly to the accessibility that many individuals with disabilities and other life challenges have to our programs and services. We, who share our days with individuals who are reliant on your compassion and financial support, thank you for more than 50 years of friendship and commitment supporting those in our communities with disabilities.

BRALEY & WELLINGTON INSURANCE AGENCY CORP.

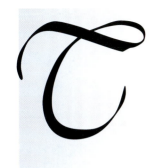

The Braley & Wellington Insurance Agency Corp. has grown over the last 35 years by joining with various local agencies and, in turn, growing our extended family of customers as well.

Before Braley & Wellington, they were known under the names of Estes & Johnston Insurance, Ernest Smith Insurance and Hamilton Davis Insurance. Since the birth of Braley & Wellington in the mid-1970s, the group has grown through the acquisitions of Greendale Insurance Agency, Malmstead Insurance Agency and, most recently in the late 1990s, the H.B. Conant Agency in Auburn and the C.D. Whitney Agency in Millbury.

The three agency locations are conveniently, not to mention intentionally, located in street-level offices with abundant parking. Although they are a professional insurance agency, with more than 200 years of experience cumulatively, they have never lost sight of the customer. The company's goal is to provide expert service, quality products and sound advice in a warm and friendly environment.

"Our approach is to treat our clients as partners," says Parker Wellington, president and CEO of Braley & Wellington Insurance Agency. "Sooner or later, things happen beyond our control. By preparing our customers for potential claims in advance and placing their interests first, we can minimize the loss and protect their future. That's our primary mission.

"We want our customers to have peace of mind, knowing that someone is looking out for them," says Wellington, "and that someone is us."

The Braley Wellington Group is a full-service insurance organization providing assistance with personal and commercial insurance needs as well as financial services.

They represent many reputable insurance carriers who offer products for any type of insurance necessity. The Personal Lines Department has extensive experience with all types of homeowners' insurance, including high-value homes, personal, automobile, boat insurance, coverage for recreational vehicles of all types as well as personal umbrellas. The personal account executives pride themselves on knowing their customers and treating them the way they would want to be treated. A majority of our customers are third- and fourth-generation patrons, and they enjoy the relationships we have formed. In addition to offering a service, the company takes pleasure in learning from the various experiences of the extended customer family.

On the commercial side, Braley & Wellington insures businesses ranging from one person to operations with hundreds of locations. Since the 1980s, Braley & Wellington has specialized in insuring petroleum marketers and environmental risks with expertise and accuracy. Each client gets specialized treatment depending on their unique operation and related risk. The company is highly involved with the trade associations for this market and makes it their goal to keep up-to-date with the rules and regulations of the industry.

In addition to niche concentrations, they are representative of many insurance carriers that thrive on serving businesses of all types. They have relationships with contractors, restaurants, manufacturers, distributors — you name it, they can help. The commercial staff has been serving the business operations of insureds throughout Central Massachusetts and beyond for many years and understand the needs of each account.

LEFT: BRALEY & WELLINGTON OFFICE, 44 PARK AVE., WORCESTER
BELOW: C.D. WHITNEY AGENCY LOCATED AT 112 ELM ST., MILLBURY

When Howard G. Freeman started the Jamesbury Co. in 1954, he did not realize that his idea for improving valves would have such a dramatic effect on so many industries. The innovation of utilizing newly developed polymers for valve sealing, coupled with quarter-turn technology, led to Jamesbury becoming the No. 1-brand valve in North America. It has since expanded to become a leading global brand as part of a large international company.

In 1954, Freeman, along with his brother Julian S. Freeman and businessman Saul I. Reck, started the business that became one of the leading companies in Central Massachusetts. The company was named after Jamesbury Street in Worcester, the street where Freeman lived.

Freeman began the company with an understanding that his innovative design would not initially be of interest to the U.S. government and the large utilities and manufacturers of the day, so he focused on providing valves to growing industries that sprouted up after World War II. He shared an innovative vision with many of the entrepreneurs who also started companies during that era and later became industry leaders.

Eventually in the 1960s, Jamesbury did supply valves to the agencies that Freeman thought would be slow to adopt them. The U.S. Navy used Jamesbury ball valves in submarines that carried nuclear weapons, large utilities utilized them in fuel management and steam, chemical producers utilized them in the most critical services and later NASA adopted them for use in the Shuttle launches.

During its 50-year history, the company has produced valves as small as 1/2 inch in diameter as well as massive valves with a 66-inch diameter. The valves range in price today from $25 to automated valve systems that total $250,000.

Though times have changed in the global valve markets, one thing has stood the test of time — the company's commitment to its employees and customers.

The company stresses values of honesty, integrity and a strong work ethic. These values are witnessed every day in its employees. These values have guided the company from its local routes in Central Massachusetts to now being part of the global entity of Metso Corporation.

There have been many successes that have contributed to the company's long history. To continue that success Jamesbury has developed operations and sales offices around the world to serve its growing customer base.

Jamesbury has a 170,000-square-foot facility in Shrewsbury which houses state-of-the-art machines, which produce thousands of valves per year. They maintain a research and development center in Shrewsbury, which continues to develop innovative products to maintain Jamesbury's technological edge.

JAMESBURY VALVES ARE UTILIZED WORLDWIDE IN APPLICATIONS RANGING FROM PULP AND PAPER, OIL REFINING AND CHEMICAL PRODUCTION — AND ALSO ON THE SPACE SHUTTLE

Ownership has changed hands only twice during the company's long history, and through the changes the company has remained committed to creating a quality product, providing great customer service and developing innovative products.

"While our vision and values laid the foundation for our success, it is our employees and community that makes a milestone of this magnitude a reality," said President John Quinlivan, while noting Jamesbury's 50th anniversary.

At that 50th anniversary celebration in 2004, more than 500 local workers, their families, as well as retired workers and their families, attended — showing the company's life-long commitment to its family of workers.

"Jamesbury is more than a local company, which has prospered over time to a global player. It is a testament to the many local people who shared Howard Freeman's vision and made it a reality," Quinlivan noted.

LEOMINSTER CREDIT UNION

hen Leominster Credit Union (LCU) opened its doors in 1954, founders believed in a commitment to community. In 1953, a group of young men of Italian ancestry decided to create a financial institution that would enable local people to receive personal loans at reasonable rates. With $2,000, they opened Leominster Credit Union. After only one year in business, the credit union had 40 members and offered share accounts, Christmas Club accounts and loans.

More than 50 years later, LCU offers a full range of financial services including deposit and loan accounts and technology-based services including Internet banking, bill pay and e-statements to North Central Massachusetts residents and small business owners. By staying on the cutting edge of technology, offering innovative products and exemplary member service, LCU has expanded beyond Leominster, its city of birth, and boasts five additional branches in Worcester, Holden, Clinton, Sterling and North Leominster. Outstanding member service remains the hallmark of LCU's mission.

The community commitment principle on which the credit union was founded is as strong as ever and evidenced by the credit union's support of two high school branches at Wachusett Regional High School in Holden and Clinton High School. These high school programs not only teach youngsters about checking accounts and car loans, but serve as a way to promote financial literacy and responsibility among high school students. Many students at these schools take advantage of summer internships available at the credit union. And, a few have been offered full-time employment at LCU. The credit union also supports educational initiatives for younger students. All About Banking is a program presented to fourth-graders at the Houghton School in Sterling and Saving Makes Cents is offered to students at Leominster's Johnny Appleseed School.

Leominster Credit Union prides itself on being a good corporate citizen, a good neighbor and an effective community leader. Staff and management are visible in local non-profit organizations, offering counsel on financial issues and volunteering person-

al time to causes important to all of us. This commitment to community is why generations of members have trusted Leominster Credit Union with their financial needs.

ABOVE: LEOMINSTER CREDIT UNION'S WORCESTER BRANCH AT 910 WEST BOYLSTON ST. (RTE. 12) OPENED IN 1999 TO SERVE THE FINANCIAL NEEDS OF WORCESTER-AREA RESIDENTS
LEFT: LCU PRESIDENT JACK CAULFIELD AND WORCESTER BRANCH MANAGER SANDRA COLLINS GREET A NEW MEMBER

MOUNT WACHUSETT COMMUNITY COLLEGE

ount Wachusett Community College's mission is to be innovative in academic programming and community and business involvement. This ensures the continuation of a 40-year legacy of offering an affordable, high-quality college education to residents of North Central Massachusetts and beyond. In the coming years, students will benefit from innovative initiatives in dental hygiene, early childhood development, child health and safety, civic engagement and renewable energy — enhancements to the college's more than 40 associate's degrees and certificates.

Mount Wachusett Community College's support of student success ranges from its caring, dynamic professors to free tutoring and to an honors program. In addition, the college encourages students to enrich their academic endeavors with hands-on training through service-learning projects and internships, as well as involvement in student clubs. Students can take advantage of weekend, on-line, non-credit, and accelerated options for added convenience.

Mount Wachusett Community College also helps area businesses meet their workforce training goals. The college customizes training to address each business's unique needs, to fit their schedule and to meet their expectations. Each year the college provides training to more than 2,000 people. The college stays abreast of local economic changes through participation in area Chambers of Commerce and other civic organizations.

Based on a 2004 Massachusetts Community Colleges economic impact report, Mount Wachusett Community College's annual impact on North Central Massachusetts is $72.1 million. A recent five-year study of the college's graduates showed that 85 percent are employed, with 80 percent in a job related to their program of study. Clearly, at Mount Wachusett Community College, North Central Massachusetts residents can start nearby on a path to success and go far. *www.mwcc.edu*

MOUNT WACHUSETT COMMUNITY COLLEGE'S MAIN CAMPUS IN GARDNER

FITCHBURG STATE COLLEGE

magine a top-flight college where you can take undergraduate, graduate or continuing education classes at a price you can afford, with an exceptional faculty that will help you realize your potential and reach your goals.

Imagine yourself at Fitchburg State College. For more than 100 years we've been one of New England's most respected colleges. You've got big dreams for your future, and a Fitchburg State education will go a long way toward making them a reality. At Fitchburg State, you'll find small classes, personal attention and plenty of choices. We offer more than 20 majors and 60 tracks and minors, as well as on-line courses and the latest in technological advances.

We believe in educating students to succeed now and in the future. In addition to acquiring a well-rounded liberal arts background and specialized knowledge in your major or professional area, you'll have ample opportunities to develop and enhance your problem-solving, decision-making and leadership skills.

Internships, research projects, alumni networking — Fitchburg State offers so many ways to get a head start on a career. And while you're preparing for your future, you'll also be enjoying a vibrant college experience — getting into discussions with friends, taking in a concert, playing sports at our new recreation center and outdoor fields, doing volunteer work or singing in the school choir.

You'll find everything you're looking for — and more — at Fitchburg State.

FOR MORE THAN A CENTURY, FITCHBURG STATE COLLEGE HAS BEEN PROVIDING HIGH-QUALITY, AFFORDABLE EDUCATION TO CITIZENS OF THE COMMONWEALTH AND BEYOND

QUINSIGAMOND COMMUNITY COLLEGE

or more than 40 years, Quinsigamond Community College has provided opportunities for a first-rate education and personal growth to thousands of area men and women.

The college offers preparation for immediate entry into a career field or for transfer to bachelor's-level programs at four-year colleges and universities. It also offers numerous opportunities for personal and cultural awareness through a variety of non-credit seminars and workshops.

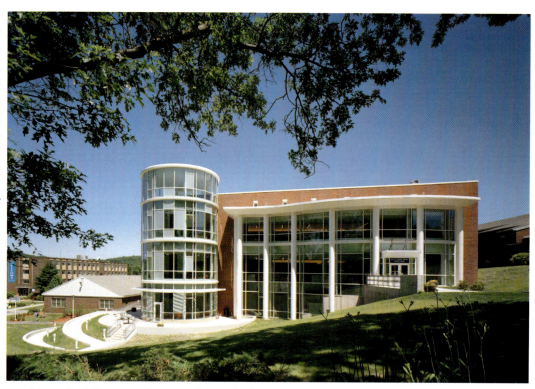

Quinsigamond was established in 1963 to provide access to higher education for residents in Central Massachusetts. In 42 years, the college's enrollment has grown from fewer than 300 to more than 7,000 full-time and part-time day and evening students. More than 70 associate's degree and certificate career choices reflect the needs of the communities it serves.

Quinsigamond Community College endeavors to meet the region's educational needs through a comprehensive selection of transfer, career and special needs courses and programs. Students can choose to seek immediate employment or transfer to a four-year college or university. QCC offers a wide variety of academic programming leading to associate's degrees or certificates in the fields of Technology, Business, Health Care, Liberal Arts and Human Services. In addition, its Continuing Education Division offers more than 300 non-credit courses, seminars and workshops, with many available on-line. The Division can also assist companies with specialized or custom-designed programming in meeting their workforce development training needs.

Few colleges have as profound an impact on the Greater Worcester area as Quinsigamond. In addition to the students it serves each year, the college provides a powerful resource for businesses and professionals in the region. Quinsigamond works to build a thriving local community through outreach programs, direct community presence and through its off-site locations, including QCC College at City Square (100 Front St.), its Hotel and Restaurant Program at the Worcester Senior Center, its Automotive Technology Program in Upton, and its Southbridge class offerings at Southbridge High School. The college also hosts forums and events that give a voice to the cultural, social and economic interests of its students, faculty and community.

Quinsigamond's flexible admissions policy, affordable cost and extensive financial-aid program have made a college education possible for thousands of men and women. The educational experience at Quinsigamond is first-rate. The classroom and laboratory facilities are well-equipped. And the support services for students are among the best anywhere.

Quinsigamond Community College exists for one purpose — to help realize the potential of its students, its staff and the community by offering a quality education at an affordable cost.

ABOVE: HARRINGTON LEARNING CENTER AND ALDEN LIBRARY

BELOW: (L-R) QCC STUDENTS JOEL JEAN-CLAUDE, TIA HOUDE AND RUMIANA PAVLOVA

THE CENTRAL MASSACHUSETTS AND WORCESTER COUNTY CONVENTION AND VISITORS BUREAU

The Central Massachusetts and Worcester County Convention and Visitors Bureau, established in 1967, is the state-appointed Regional Tourist Council, representing the 58 communities in our area, the largest geographic land mass in the Commonwealth. Our mission is to market, promote and enhance the image of our region, drawing domestic and international visitors in ever-increasing numbers.

Central Massachusetts is home to rich cultural diversity, natural beauty, well-known family attractions, fine dining and world-class hotels. It encompasses five distinct areas: Greater Worcester, Sturbridge and the Brookfields, North County (or the Johnny Appleseed Trail), the Blackstone Valley and the Metro-West Area. You'll find such well-known sites as Old Sturbridge Village, Wachusett Mountain, the Blackstone Valley Heritage Corridor, Salem Cross Inn, Worcester Art Museum, Higgins Armory, the DCU Center, Mechanics Hall and much more. Tourism in Central Massachusetts continues to grow with every year, averaging 1.9 million visitors annually.

Worcester is Massachusetts' second-largest city, offering outstanding cultural, entertainment and recreational activities, including a number of major museums. The Worcester Art Museum — the third-largest in New England — features a permanent collection of more than 30,000 works, including those of Renoir, Monet and John Singer Sargent. Higgins Armory features the largest on-display collection of Medieval and Renaissance armor in the Western Hemisphere. The EcoTarium features environmental exhibits, wildlife, a tree canopy walkway and a planetarium on 60 acres of woodlands and wetlands for visitors to explore and enjoy.

Worcester is also home to a magnificent convention center and performance site, the DCU Center, the No. 3-ranked venue in the world by *Billboard* magazine. The city also boasts 10 colleges and universities, including the College of the Holy Cross College, Clark University, WPI (Worcester Polytechnic Institute), the Massachusetts College of Pharmacy and Health Sciences and the University of Massachusetts Medical School.

North Worcester County, the birthplace of American folk hero John Chapman, features The Johnny Appleseed Trail. Lakes, mountains and parks abound, along with picturesque towns and villages, each featuring events and attractions year-round.

Described as "History with a View," the Blackstone River Valley National Heritage Corridor, just south of Worcester, is the birthplace of America's Industrial Revolution. Today, the river runs clear and wildlife is abundant, available to anyone with a bicycle, canoe, cross-country skis or a good pair of sneakers.

Sturbridge and the Brookfields, in the southwest corner of Worcester County, offer a glimpse of America at an even earlier time. Dotted with antiques shops, fine examples of Victorian architecture and many wonderful restaurants, visitors from far and wide are attracted to this area's crown jewel — Old Sturbridge Village — where mid-19th century New England life is lovingly recreated.

Central Massachusetts is rich in history, natural beauty and culture, offering something for everyone. It truly is the "Heart of New England," and that's why the Central Massachusetts and Worcester County Convention and Visitors Bureau urges you to "Follow Your Heart!" and make it a part of your leisure plans in the near future.

For more information, please visit us online at *www.worcester.org*, or call 1-800-231-7557.

FROM A MEETING AND CONVENTION DESTINATION TO WORLD-CLASS MUSEUMS, FINE HOTELS AND HISTORIC B&Bs, SHOPPING, RECREATION, FINE DINING AND ENTERTAINMENT, "CENTRAL MASSACHUSETTS — THE HEART OF NEW ENGLAND" HAS IT ALL

YOUTH OPPORTUNITIES UPHELD, INC. — Y.O.U., INC.

I n 2005, Y.O.U. Inc. celebrated 35 years of guiding young people and families to brighter futures. It also celebrated the evolution of a small program designed to help kids coming through the juvenile justice system into one of the largest and most respected social service programs in Central Massachusetts.

As late as the 1960s, Central Massachusetts did not have a juvenile court. Youthful offenders — including kids who simply skipped school or ran away from home — were funneled through the adult criminal justice system. In 1969, through the efforts of Carol A. Schmidt and other community leaders, a juvenile court was established in Worcester.

Even as it celebrated its success, this coalition recognized the need to provide services to the young people coming through the juvenile court. So in 1970, they founded Youth Opportunities Upheld — better known as Y.O.U. Inc. — and selected Maurice J. "Moe" Boisvert, then a newly minted social worker, as its first director.

Thirty-five years later, Boisvert continues to lead an agency that has grown exponentially and today provides cutting-edge services to 7,000 children, teens and families navigating a maze of complex problems. These services are delivered through more than 30 programs at a number of sites in Central Massachusetts. Many of the programs are community-based. Others are residential. Some focus on education and work skills. Still others offer life-changing counseling and therapy. All share a single goal — to guide young people and their families to brighter futures.

Y.O.U. Inc.'s community-based services provide an impressive array of innovative programs. Mentoring extends a lifeline to juveniles in conflict with the law. After-school programs help children and teens with anger management, academics, and peer and family relationships. A clinical team helps stabilize families in crisis. For juvenile fire setters, there's a treatment program. For teens picked up by the police, there are emergency placements. And for children and teens who need more support than their families or the traditional foster care system can provide, there's a special foster care program.

Every year, more than 600 children and teens spend time in one of Y.O.U. Inc.'s residential programs. Each residence is designed for young people of different ages, with different problems and different needs. Cottage Hill Academy mixes education and clinical services with life skills, recreation and other essentials for challenged teen girls. The Joy and Robert Wetzel Children's Center operates as an effective alternative to inpatient psychiatric hospitalization

ABOVE: SURROUNDED BY GANGS AND VIOLENCE, THE POSTONS ONCE CONSIDERED COLLEGE AN IMPOSSIBLE DREAM. BUT BY TAKING ADVANTAGE OF Y.O.U. INC. PROGRAMS, DAMIAN (FRONT RIGHT) AND MONIQUE (RIGHT) ARE NOW STUDENTS AT BROWN UNIVERSITY AND WHEELOCK COLLEGE, RESPECTIVELY
LEFT: A 1970 *SUNDAY TELEGRAM* PHOTO CAPTURES JUDGE LUCIAN MANZI AND CAROL SCHMIDT EXCHANGING CONGRATULATIONS OVER THE ESTABLISHMENT OF WORCESTER'S FIRST JUVENILE COURT (REPRINTED WITH PERMISSION OF THE WORCESTER *TELEGRAM & GAZETTE*)

for children from 7 to 18. Two residences provide homeless teen mothers with parenting and life skills. Another cares for young children. Each home offers its young residents a warm environment and a caring staff, as well as the structure, programs and intensive intervention that enable them to grow, change and reintegrate into the community.

In a competitive world, education and work skills are essential to success. Each year, young people with histories of school failure experience success in Y.O.U. Inc.'s special education programs. Adults and young people who have dropped out of school gain the skills they need to achieve goals that once seemed beyond their reach. Through a collaborative program with the Worcester Public Schools and Clark University, low-income, first-generation high school students are realizing their dream of attending college.

At counseling centers in Worcester, Southbridge and Gardner, Y.O.U. Inc. offers individual, family and group therapy as well as diagnostic and support services. A pioneering new program offers mental health services for preschoolers. As licensed mental health and substance abuse clinics, these centers also serve as training sites for counselors and social workers.

Y.O.U. Inc. also collaborates with the state Department of Social Services and other social services agencies to deliver needed services for at-risk youth and families in Central Massachusetts.

What accounts for Y.O.U. Inc.'s growth? And its record of success? To President and CEO Maurice Boisvert, it's always been about seeing a need and finding a way to respond. To that basic formula, add a skilled, caring staff and a seasoned management team. Then factor in the community — a diverse and dedicated board, impressive corporate and foundation support, generous individual donors, faith-based organizations, and many individuals and community groups who give of their time and talent.

And how is success measured? Some outcomes, such as graduation rates, can be measured objectively.

Others, such as family stabilization, occur over a longer period of time and are more difficult to quantify. And then there are all the bad things that don't happen — the teen who stays out of trouble with the law, the student who doesn't drop out of school, the child who avoids inpatient psychiatric hospitalization. And always, there's the gold standard — lives where Y.O.U. Inc.'s transforming influence is clearly visible.

Sarah Carey is a case in point. In 1982, Sarah was a homeless 13-year-old who had just run from one more in a long line of foster homes. "They believed in me when I could not believe in myself," she says of the people she encountered at Y.O.U. Inc. Today, Sarah is married, with a child and a stable life. She is also a member of Y.O.U. Inc.'s board, making a difference in the next generation of young lives.

For Y.O.U. Inc., success is not something to savor so much as a spur to future achievement. The agency's Guidelines for the Future — developed with input from all its stakeholders — establishes goals for innovation, growth and services that reach even more children and families and transform even more lives. It's an ambitious agenda. But based on the first 35 years, it's entirely realistic.

ABOVE: MAURICE "MOE" BOISVERT HAS BEEN AT THE HELM OF Y.O.U. INC. SINCE ITS LAUNCH IN 1970 RIGHT: AT ONE TIME, SARAH CAREY WAS A HOMELESS TEEN. TODAY, SHE'S MARRIED AND TAKING TIME FROM A SUCCESSFUL CAREER TO RAISE NATHANIEL. AS A MEMBER OF Y.O.U. INC.'S BOARD, SHE'S ALSO GIVING BACK AND MAKING A DIFFERENCE

LAMOUREUX PAGANO ASSOCIATES, ARCHITECTS

Lamoureux Pagano Associates was founded in 1969 by Richard Lamoureux, dedicated to providing quality design and the highest level of professional service. Through adherence to its founding principles, Lamoureux Pagano Associates has grown to become one of the most prominent architectural firms in the state. The firm employs seven registered architects supported by 25 state-of-the-art computer stations utilized for all aspects of design, document preparation and construction administration. Well known for the diversity of its portfolio, the company has completed new buildings and renovations spanning the full spectrum of small residential projects through large new multi-million-dollar buildings.

The architects of Lamoureux Pagano Associates believe that inspiration for design is found in the site and client's program. With the owner fully involved in the design process from the statement of objectives through occupancy, the completed work reflects the client's objectives and opportunities presented by the site. The firm's consistent commitment to quality design and the highest level of professional service has earned them the reputation as one of the most respected architectural firms in Central Massachusetts.

For more than 30 years, Lamoureux Pagano Associates has earned numerous awards providing architectural services to many of Massachusetts' best known businesses and institutions. Design Excellence and Preservation awards have been presented for the Becker College Academic Center, the Worcester Academy Student Center, Quinsigamond Elementary School in Worcester and the International Golf Club in Bolton, Mass.

Among a series of Worcester commissions, Lamoureux Pagano Associates was selected to design the municipality's largest capital project to date — the flagship Worcester Technical High School.

The firm has completed projects including sophisticated corporate research and office facilities, commercial buildings for business and industry, transportation and parking facilities, educational and municipal structures and housing. In addition to working with municipalities throughout the state, Lamoureux Pagano Associates has worked with major private-sector institutional, industrial and commercial businesses.

The firm's success has been built on long-standing professional relationships in Central Massachusetts. In return, members of the firm have made commitments to support numerous local organizations by volunteering in leadership positions for the American Institute of Architects, Preservation Worcester, Higgins Armory Museum, Hope Lodge, and Mechanics Hall, among others. While continuing to provide architectural/engineering services for residential, commercial and institutional buildings, the firm is expanding its services to include project management. Firmly rooted in the community, Lamoureux Pagano Associates is committed to remain in Worcester.

ABOVE: QUINSIGAMOND SCHOOL RESTORATION AND ADDITIONS RECOGNIZED FOR DESIGN EXCELLENCE BY THE MASSACHUSETTS HISTORICAL COMMISSION BELOW: WORCESTER TECHNICAL HIGH SCHOOL

RAINBOW CHILD DEVELOPMENT CENTER INC.

The Rainbow Child Development Center Inc. was founded as a non-profit childcare corporation in 1972. Families living in Plumley Village (a subsidized housing development in Worcester) and State Mutual Life Assurance Company (owner of Plumley Village) worked together to establish the agency. In its first year of operation, the Center cared for 24 children in its Family Child Care and Preschool programs. Today, the Center serves approximately 250 children and operates a School Age program as well. All programs are licensed by the State of Massachusetts.

The Center's mission is to provide education and therapeutic services to children and families in a safe and nurturing environment, where children learn and grow to reach their individual potential, and families receive encouragement and services to support their children's development. All programs operate from 7:30 a.m. to 5:30 p.m., Monday through Friday, 52 weeks a year.

The Rainbow's Family Child Care program provides care to children ages 6 weeks to 3 years in the homes of licensed providers, which are located throughout Worcester. All providers are Rainbow employees, each having 4 to 6 children in their care.

Rainbow's Preschool program serves children ages 2.9 to 5 in five classroom settings. The preschool operates an open-education, language-based program that supports children's growth in all areas of development. The program is nationally accredited by the National Association for the Education of Young Children (NAEYC).

The agency's School Age program, for children ages 5-13, operates at Belmont Community and City View schools and at its Edward Street location during the school year and provides full day service during school vacation weeks and the summer. The focus of the School Age program is an educational, cultural and recreational curriculum. During the summer months, Rainbow leases space at the Mohegan Boy Scout Council's Treasure Valley Boy Scout Reservation, where children are bused each day for a "fresh air" summer camp experience.

Rainbow provides supportive services to children and families by collaborating with a number of community agencies. Services include early intervention, speech development therapy, play and art therapy, and individual and group counseling services. Rainbow is a participant in the "Together for Kids" (TFK) pilot project whose mission is to provide mental health services to children with behavioral problems as well as providing guidance to their families. The Center is an active participant, in collaboration with the Worcester Public Schools, in the Worcester Community Partnership. Rainbow also enjoys a positive relationship with Worcester's higher-education institutions whose students participate in volunteer, service learning, internship and project opportunities.

In March 2005, Rainbow opened the doors of its new home at 10 Edward St. For close to 100 years, the building functioned as a safe haven for children and women under the Temporary Home and Day Nursery and Edward Street Day Care Center organizations.

Now, Rainbow Child Development Center Inc. continues the legacy of services and programs for Worcester's children and families. This wonderful new location allows the Center to provide additional classroom space, more functional office space, and meeting space for the board of directors and parent/staff workshops. The additional space allows the agency to consider other innovative programming opportunities for children and families as well.

Rainbow has launched a fund-raising campaign to provide for renovations and improvements to its new Edward Street location. In its new facility, the Center looks forward to continuing its services to Worcester's children and families for many years to come.

THE BRIDGE OF CENTRAL MASSACHUSETTS INC.

The Bridge of Central Massachusetts Inc. provides state-of-the-art human services to individuals and families across the area.

The Bridge consists of 33 programs that provide human services to a diverse clientele. The Bridge was founded in 1973 in two separate areas: Westboro and Worcester. In Westboro, following two years of grassroots fundraising, The Bridge opened its first program; a group home for eight boys who were discharged from the soon-to-be closed Lyman School.

Meanwhile, a few miles west, an after-school program opened in 1973 on the grounds of Worcester State Hospital. Designed as a means to assist severely disturbed adolescents, this program (founded by Barent Walsh, Ph.D., Paul Rosen, Ph.D. and a small Board of Directors) became known as the Community Treatment Center (CTC). In time, the CTC's roster of programs evolved to include G. Stanley Hall School, a special-education school located in Worcester.

From 1974-1997, The Bridge and CTC worked separately to serve similar populations in two different areas. In general, the programs were small group homes based in the community as part of the growing deinstitutionalization movement. People served were either individuals with emotional disturbance and mental illness or mental retardation.

In 1997, the two agencies merged to form the new, improved Bridge of Central Massachusetts. That merger resulted in a stronger Board of Trustees, more sophisticated and effective services, enhanced financial stability and increased fundraising capabilities.

Following the merger, the Board of Trustees, led by J. Christopher Collins, were committed to search for a more centrally located space for agency headquarters and larger quarters for the G. Stanley Hall School. The search resulted in the purchase and renovation of a 29,000-square-foot condominium in a former factory on Worcester's West Side. The new G. Stanley Hall School and Bridge headquarters opened on Mann Street in Worcester in 2003.

During the past three decades, The Bridge has served generations of people with diverse needs, has successfully integrated them into the community, and has helped to markedly enhance their quality of life. The mission of The Bridge is fundamentally important: We advocate for individuals to become full partners in the experience of lifelong learning, meaningful relationships, productive work and community living.

Since 1973, thousands of children, adults and

senior citizens have benefited from services provided by The Bridge. Recognized for our specialized therapies, our excellent reputation with funders and families alike is due to our clinical sophistication and client-centered approach. Treating clients who may be suicidal or self-injurious, or those who have not succeeded in other treatment programs, are two of The Bridge's many strengths.

The Bridge has 33 program sites in Metrowest (Hudson and Marlboro) and Central Mass. (Gardner, Northboro, Southboro, Southbridge, Westboro, West Brookfield, Worcester and

Webster) that provide special education, residential treatment, supported housing and homeless services.

The agency motto: *Diverse Challenges — Creative Solutions* demonstrates our commitment to fostering an environment that respects and celebrates diversity. We are an organization of 350 employees and more than a quarter of our staff are minorities. Our clientele is also diverse as to race, age and income. Although their profiles and needs are different, all come to The Bridge for help facing challenges. Our highly trained staff of teachers, social workers, psychologists, physicians, counselors, nurses and other professionals (89% of whom live in Worcester County) are here to help 24 hours a day.

There are many important milestones in the organization's history, among the most prominent is our accreditation by the Council on Accreditation, which attests that the agency meets the highest national standards and is delivering the best quality services to the community. We are also proud that in 2004, The Bridge's Grove Street Adolescent Residence in Westboro received the American Psychiatric Association's Gold Award — the most prestigious public sector award in the country.

Other significant markers include the development of a network of child and adolescent residential services; the implementation of evidence-based Dialectical Behavior Therapy in eight programs; the establishment of an array of housing options for individuals with developmental disabilities; provi-

sion of services for the homeless; the operation of the Safe Homes drop-in center; and our status as a housing authority — which provides many housing options to our clients and the community at large.

Earning the trust and respect of funders and those we serve has helped the agency survive turbulent times during state budget crises. That respect is well-earned, as the committed eight-person leadership team has many years of service and dedication to The Bridge. Headed by Executive Director Barent Walsh, Ph.D., The Bridge leadership team has successfully worked to increase community acceptance of people with special needs.

Only 30 years ago, many of the individuals now served by The Bridge would have lived their lives locked up in large institutions. Today, with the support of dedicated staff, they live in small homes or in their own apartments in residential neighborhoods. The Bridge has taken a leadership role in the movement to successfully integrate people into the community where they have jobs, volunteer work and friends. With the help of new medications and treatment options, people with serious emotional disturbance, mental illness and mental retardation now enjoy lives of hope and meaning.

As we look to our next decade, our vision is one of steady growth in providing our principal services of residential care, supported housing and special education. With the support of our community partners, civic leaders and staff, The Bridge will continue to find ways to improve the quality of life for the children, adults and families we serve.

The Holden Landmark Corp. was launched in the bicentennial year of 1976, not with the fanfare of our nation's birthday but certainly with the goal of perpetuating the great American tradition of excellence in journalism.

The company began with a single newspaper, *The Landmark*, which grew from a bimonthly publication covering Holden, to a thriving weekly that also reports the news from the towns of Paxton, Princeton, Rutland and Sterling.

It is *the* source of hometown information for people in the Wachusett region, who rely on *The Landmark* for comprehensive reporting on area politics, police, schools and sports, and lively features chronicling the people and events that give these communities their unique flavor and create the headlines.

The newspaper industry has recognized these efforts, with *The Landmark* earning numerous awards for writing and photography from the likes of The New England Press Association, The National Newspaper Association and Suburban Newspapers of America.

In 2002, the company acquired *The Community Journal*, which at the time served the towns of Ashburnham, Ashby and Westminster. Recently, the paper added Townsend to its coverage area, giving that town the same high-quality journalism *Community Journal* readers have come to expect.

Each Friday, *The Community Journal* hits the streets with the most thorough coverage of local news, sports, politics and town events — with reporting that's aggressive, lively and essential to its readership. The paper's design is vibrant and welcoming, and the communities it serves regard the "*CJ*" as the week's must-read.

Also under the company's aegis is *Bay State Parent* magazine, a staple in the lives of parents throughout Worcester County. Reaching more than 100,000 readers each month, *Bay State Parent* delivers the most up-to-date information on parenting issues in Worcester County and Metrowest. Covering the hot topics of health care, schools, events and activities, plus special features

on places to go — including our popular Massachusetts Field Trip Guide — party planning and parental resources, *Bay State Parent* is synchronized with the everyday lives of its readers. *Bay State Parent* also has made a splash in the publishing industry, earning awards from The New England Press Association and Parenting Publications of America for its compelling features, photography and design. In 2004, *Bay State Parent* was cited as the Best Parenting Publication by Suburban Newspapers of America, a national trade association with more than 2,000 members.

With the opportunities and challenges of the Information Age, The Holden Landmark Corp. is spreading its wings, identifying fresh, new ways to fill its role as the conduit for first-hand local content and ideas through the Internet. The company currently publishes four Web sites: *the-landmark.com*, *thecommunityjournal.com*, *baystateparent.com* and *massfieldtrips.com*. Whether through print or megabytes, the reliable sharing of homespun news weaves together and builds a vital sense of community — of belonging to a larger whole — which is what communication is all about.

THE HOLDEN LANDMARK CORPORATION

PUBLISHES ON THE WEB AT:

WWW.THELANDMARK.COM

WWW.THECOMMUNITYJOURNAL.COM

WWW.BAYSTATEPARENT.COM

WWW.MASSFIELDTRIPS.COM

UNIVERSITY OF PHOENIX

n today's dynamic workplace, it is not enough to have the right degree or work experience to land a great job or earn a promotion. Employees who want to advance in their careers also must be team players with excellent communication and problem-solving skills, according to a national survey conducted by the University of Phoenix.

With its goal of providing access to education for busy adults through flexible scheduling and degree programs centered on professional goals, the University of Phoenix's focus on small interactive classes, highly personalized teaching and required student group study sessions that encourage an interactive learning model, is the ideal option for employees looking to finish or advance their education. At the University of Phoenix in Massachusetts, working adult students can earn their bachelor's or master's degrees in a number of ways — on campus, online, or using a combination of both, called FlexNet.

The Central Massachusetts Campus of the University of Phoenix, conveniently located at the junction of routes 9 and 495 in Westboro, has seen explosive growth since opening in 2004 and offers the following degrees: Bachelor of Science in Business Management; Bachelor of Science in Business Administration; Bachelor of Science in Information Technology; Master's in Business Administration; Master's in Business Administration/Global Management; and Master's in Business Administration/Technology Management.

"It is not enough to have the relevant skills and experience," explains Robert K. Adler, campus director for the University of Phoenix's Massachusetts campuses. "Those who want to hold on to their jobs and move up the career ladder must be able to present the right attitude, communicate well with their peers and work in teams."

According to the poll, executives said the most important skills employees need to succeed in today's workplace are communication (96%), followed by learning aptitude/desire to grow (95%), collaboration and teamwork (93%) and creative problem-solving (92%).

At the University of Phoenix, education focuses on the whole person. Programs are tailored to specific professions or industries, such as business, human services and information technology, but its academic environment also incorporates assignments which enable students to practice leading and following, hone teamwork and discussion skills, and use critical thinking and problem-solving at their present jobs, even as they complete their degrees.

When asked to rank the importance of four distinct employee attributes, participants rated personal skills, such as attitude and chemistry (97%) and professional skills, including communication and presentation abilities (93A%), higher than work experience or the right education (78% and 68%, respectively).

However, this does not mean formal education is not highly regarded. In fact, more than half of those surveyed (51%) favor continuous improvement and the updating of skills through education and training. Nearly 57% of the respondents offer tuition reimbursement to employees seeking to enhance their skills.

Adler concludes, "These statistics tells us that today's employees, particularly those in the fastest-growing industries, are expected to adapt quickly to industry changes and differing roles within their respective organizations and post-secondary institutions have to keep up, too, adapting their learning strategies to meet the ever-changing demands of a workplace that has become increasingly complex and global."

The University of Phoenix, with locations in Westboro, Braintree and Burlington, is a bricks-and-mortar school that offers undergraduate and graduate business courses. New classes begin every month of the year and course schedules are all about flexibility.

FALLON COMMUNITY HEALTH PLAN

ased in the heart of Massachusetts, Fallon Community Health Plan has been providing health care services to the community since 1977. FCHP started out as the very first HMO in Central Massachusetts and quickly made its mark on health care in the state and the country.

As the health care industry has progressed in the last decade, FCHP has evolved into a health care services organization, uniquely positioned as both a health plan and a provider of care. And it continues the process of building a company that strives to go above and beyond its customers' expectations.

What is Fallon Community Health Plan today? It's a multi-faceted organization committed on many levels to the communities it serves: it offers a large portfolio of products and services to help employers manage health care costs; it provides extensive benefits, wellness features and clinical programs to promote members' health; it crafts provider networks that extend throughout Massachusetts—and beyond; it collaborates with key provider partners to create and use technology to promote safe health care; it gives support for critical services in the community; and, unlike other health plans, it also is a direct provider of care, an extraordinary role that gives FCHP an unparalleled perspective to develop better clinical and financial solutions.

In 2004, Fallon Community Health Plan embarked on a new course that has accelerated its transformation from a Central Massachusetts group model HMO to a mixed-model health care services company with members throughout the state and beyond. This redefinition of FCHP's business identity has been guided by its new board of directors—business and community leaders from throughout Massachusetts—whose diversity of thought and expertise will help the organization face 21st-century challenges.

With this strong board leadership and a tremendously committed and caring workforce of more than 500 employees, FCHP has successfully responded to its customers' appeal for a broader network and more flexible, cost-effective products.

One of FCHP's most notable recent achievements was the substantial and focused growth of its HMO network. FCHP more than doubled its network to over 12,000 providers and 41 hospitals statewide. In

particular, FCHP built new relationships with many very popular provider systems from the Merrimack Valley, the MetroWest region, the Route 128 corridor, the South Shore and the Pioneer Valley. And it continues to carefully grow the network to meet its customers' needs.

FCHP also provides a unique solution in the Massachusetts health care marketplace: a health care product built exclusively around a more-defined network of high-performing providers, specifically Fallon Clinic, Acton Medical Associates, Charles River Medical Associates and Southboro Medical Group.

As the health care landscape continues to change, FCHP is poised to respond with solutions customized to suit all its customers' needs. In the year 2004 alone, Fallon Community Health Plan enhanced and developed more products and services than in all of its 27-year history. Building on its benchmark HMO products, it created a variety of benefit options that offer the time-tested reassurance, simplicity and value of an HMO, but with a greater choice of premium selections. It also introduced more comprehensive benefit options for its nationwide

THE FALLON SENIOR PLAN
WAS ONE OF THE FIRST
MEDICARE HEALTH PLANS IN
THE COUNTRY

ElderCare, based on PACE (Program of All-inclusive Care for the Elderly), a national model of care, FCHP directly provides medical care and other critical services to frail elders. Summit ElderCare, located on East Mountain Street, in Worcester, is an innovative alternative to nursing home care and, in addition, offers caregivers the support and peace of mind they need to help better manage their own life challenges. The program, previously known as Elder Service Plan, marked its 10th anniversary in 2005.

In support of Fallon Community Health Plan's mission of *making our communities healthy*, it also provides tools to help all members of its communities stay as healthy as possible in all stages of their lives. For example, FCHP's personalized programs to manage chronic illnesses such as congestive heart failure, asthma, diabetes and chronic obstructive pulmonary disease, promote real and lasting health changes while controlling costs related to care. Rather than using outside resources, FCHP chose to turn to the expertise of local, in-house nurses, who can respond more efficiently and personally to members because they live and work in the region and know its health care providers. They also offer a variety of wellness programs that support members in maintaining healthy lifestyles.

Adhering to its mission, Fallon Community Health Plan contributes more than $1 million annually to community initiatives that improve the health and well-being of residents in Central Massachusetts and beyond. FCHP gives back to the community by providing comprehensive health promotion and education programs, and by providing resources and support to organizations that improve access to medical treatment across all populations, or deliver social services to at-risk youth. In addition, FCHP sponsors events that bring communities together, like the Independence Day Celebration and summertime Movies in the Park series.

As the cost of health care continues to rise, FCHP recognizes that, for some of its members, one of the biggest barriers to receiving the right care at the right time may be a financial one. In response, FCHP recently became the first health plan in Massachusetts to eliminate its members' office visit copayments for routine physical exams, annual gynecological exams and well-child visits.

FCHP partnered with UMass Memorial Health Care and Fallon Clinic on an innovative program called SAFE Health. This exciting project will create pioneering technology that will provide real-time, confidential access to medical information that will significantly increase patient safety, improve clinical outcomes and reduce health care costs.

At the heart of all of FCHP's decisions is its members' health and well-being. As a health care services company, Fallon Community Health Plan is always standing by, prepared to respond with solutions or services, for whatever life brings.

ABOVE: FOUNDED IN 1977, FCHP PROVIDES HEALTH CARE SERVICES DESIGNED TO MEET THE UNIQUE AND CHANGING NEEDS OF ALL THEY SERVE BELOW: HIGH-QUALITY HEALTH CARE AND EXCEPTIONAL CUSTOMER SERVICE PLACE FCHP AS ONE OF THE NATION'S TOP HEALTH PLANS YEAR AFTER YEAR

PPO product, which provides access to a network of more than 450,000 providers.

Likewise, the need for diverse, cost-effective product options is equally important to FCHP's senior customers. Because of historic changes to the nation's Medicare program, this important population is faced with critical decisions about their health care coverage. FCHP has responded by offering a variety of plan options to individuals, as well as retirees of employer groups, giving them more alternatives to have the coverage they need, when they need it.

FCHP is the only health plan in the state to offer both Medicare and Medicaid plans. While their Medicare Advantage plans reassure seniors when it comes to their health, their Medicaid (MassHealth) plan provides lower-income residents of Massachusetts with the access they need to quality health care and services. And, FCHP continues to work with policymakers to find solutions that will drive universal access to health insurance for all.

A distinguishing aspect of Fallon Community Health Plan is that it is not only a health plan, but also a health care provider. Because its expertise lies in both worlds, FCHP can create clinical programs that are both top-notch and affordable. Through its Summit

BENEFIT DEVELOPMENT GROUP

enefit Development Group (BDG) knows that few things pose as big a challenge to today's business leaders as providing valued employees with attractive benefit plans while maintaining the health of their company's bottom line. This goal has been the Worcester company's focus while helping large and small area companies in a changing insurance landscape for three decades.

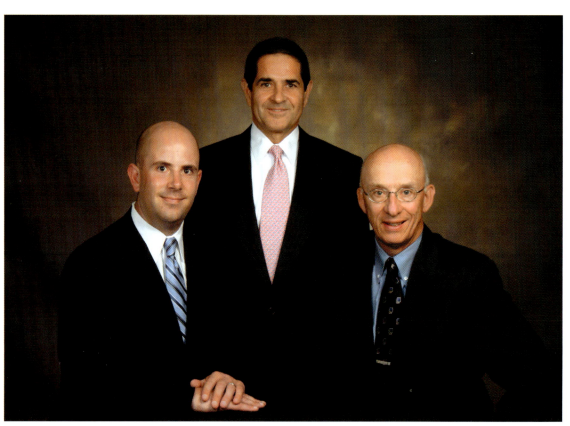

ABOVE: (L-R) CHRISTOPHER POWERS, SENIOR VICE PRESIDENT; MICHAEL TSOTSIS, PRESIDENT/CEO; AND MARK FULLER, VICE PRESIDENT

Whether guiding clients through the expansive array of options to deal with rising health insurance costs, or assuring that they get the best premiums year after year through hands-on bid negotiation, BDG develops a comprehensive employee benefits strategy tailored to each company's philosophy and direction. The process begins by getting to know each business they serve. BDG meets with clients to review their current benefit plans, assess the value to employees and establish goals and strategies for improvement. Once a plan is put in place, BDG provides ongoing analysis to make sure the benefits keep pace with changing insurance needs and shifting industry trends. They also help clients transition between carriers when necessary and communicate plan and benefit changes to employees.

Founded in 1976, the company's focus since its inception has always been to provide its clients with a broad range of group benefit services to help ensure their financial security. BDG prides itself on being a service-oriented benefits consultant whose knowledgeable staff brings to the table decades of collective experience in the management ranks of the nation's largest insurance carriers. They combine their expertise in a unique approach to serving customers. Says BDG founder and President Michael Tsotsis, a 32-year veteran of the industry, "When we get involved in a case, we are continually available. Everyone here has ownership in the case. We work to ensure that the highest level of service is maintained and keep our clients informed of industry trends."

BDG offers an extensive array of services, including strategic planning and design assistance with group benefit programs, such as group health, group life, disability and dental plans, long-term care and critical illness plans and voluntary benefit programs. Since they partner with the insurance industry's leading companies, BDG can match the best products with each client's specific needs. The staff is also well-versed in all aspects of ERISA welfare benefit plans, as well as alternative benefit products such as cafeteria plans, health saving accounts and health reimbursement plans.

BDG serves corporate clients throughout the United States that range in size from 10 employees to more than 51,000. BDG helps address employee needs in a wide range of industries, from manufacturers to hospitals and physician groups, utilities, insurance companies, municipalities, high-tech and biotech.

In today's demanding business climate, where employers rely on comprehensive benefits to attract and retain qualified employees, BDG provides the essential consulting services to get the job done.

DCU CENTER

for more than two decades, the DCU Center in Worcester has been recognized as the gathering place for people to experience the finest in entertainment, sporting events and public functions. Hailed as one of the most successful entertainment and convention facilities in the nation, the DCU Center opened its doors in September, 1982, with the legendary Frank Sinatra Inaugural Concert. Since that time, acts of all musical genres have found their way to the arena stage. From rock to rap, country to contemporary, millions of fans from all over the world have come to the DCU Center to see their favorite performers, including Madonna, Aerosmith, Garth Brooks and Keith Lockhart.

The arena features regular stops of the family shows that entertain children of all ages, including Ringling Bros. and Barnum & Bailey Circus, Sesame Street Live, Disney On Ice, Harlem Globetrotters and The Wiggles, as well as new touring products on an annual basis. It was during the mid-'80s that the arena expanded to nearly 15,000 seats and allowed audiences to witness a wide variety of memorable sporting events, including World Championship and Olympic Boxing, Professional Bull Riding, and the MIAA High School Basketball and Hockey State Finals. Since opening, the DCU Center has hosted the First and Second Rounds of the NCAA Men's Basketball Championships twice. Televised on CBS, the championships not only gave Worcester priceless national exposure, but also brought several million dollars in revenue to the region with visitors from across the nation packing restaurants and hotels. The DCU Center also holds the distinct honor of hosting NCAA Men's Ice Hockey regional tournaments more times than any other arena.

The DCU Center expanded again in 1997 with the opening of an attached state-of-the-art convention center that features panoramic views of downtown Worcester. The complex, described as an architectural gem, added 50,000 square feet of exhibit space, 11 meeting rooms, a 12,144-square-foot ballroom (the largest in Central Massachusetts) and a state-of-the-art kitchen. The convention center's 100,000-plus square feet of exhibit space is filled by consumer shows, trade shows, conventions, conferences and other public and private functions year-round.

In October 2004, as the result of a naming rights agreement between the City of Worcester and Digital Federal Credit Union (DCU) — the largest credit union headquartered in New England — the facility was renamed The DCU Center. The naming rights

partnership, a unique branding opportunity, is for a 10-year term and has a value of more than $11 million in cash and marketing benefits. Sure to enhance the venue's regional and national appeal as a true destination, ground has been broken for a new convention hotel adjacent to the facility, along with a pedestrian sky bridge — connecting the new hotel, the Worcester Municipal Parking Garage and the convention center.

Continuing to provide the best possible experience for the promoter, performer and patron, the DCU Center is owned by the City of Worcester and managed by SMG, the world's leading private management and development firm for public assembly facilities. SMG provides facility services to more than 170 venues, managing more than 10 million square feet of exhibit space and controlling more than 1.46 million entertainment seats worldwide.

THE DCU CENTER, ONE OF THE WORLD'S MOST SUCCESSFUL ENTERTAINMENT AND CONVENTION FACILITIES

WOODMEISTER CORPORATION

t's hard to imagine a more perfect example of an entrepreneurial success story than the 25-year history of Woodmeister Corporation. What started as a young man's passion for woodworking has grown at an astounding pace into a nationally renowned, multi-million-dollar business. In that short span of time, Woodmeister has not only achieved the rank and reputation of a well-established leader in the luxury home market, it has also created a whole new industry threshold for quality and craftsmanship.

While still a teenager and with a two-year woodworking apprenticeship under his belt, Ted Goodnow (company founder and CEO) began pursuing his dream of becoming a craftsman. "I loved working with my hands. I knew exactly what I wanted to do with my life, and I wanted to start doing it," Goodnow recalls. In January, 1980, he opened up a tiny shop in Worcester and began carving out a niche in the commercial and residential millwork and cabinetry market. After landing his first big kitchen contract, Goodnow was forced to move to larger quarters to complete the job. The company has grown unabated ever since.

Joined by his wife, Kim, in 1986, Goodnow gave up the hands-on work of the business and devoted all of his time to managing and growing the company. Today, with more than 135 employees and operations in both Worcester and on Nantucket, Woodmeister encompasses the entire scope of luxury custom-home renovation, restoration, expansion and construction projects — design-build, millwork, cabinetry, stairs and turnkey customer-centered service.

While Woodmeister has expanded into the luxury-home construction market, the company continues to focus on its core business of custom interiors and renovations. Its exclusive, one-of-a-kind cabinetry and millwork are second to none in the industry. "Almost right from the beginning, I knew that I wanted to create the absolute best cabinetry and millwork for people who desire the extraordinary," Goodnow says. "I always loved and admired the timelessness and beauty of Old World craftsmanship; I wanted my company to make that kind of woodwork — the kind that will last for genera-

tions and generations." Woodmeister recognizes, however, that quality is only part of the equation in meeting the needs of its clients. Affluent homeowners often want more than the best — they want exclusivity. "Our customers are searching for fresh and original ideas that will reflect their lifestyles, tastes and personalities," Goodnow says. "They want something that nobody else has, and they want it to take your breath away. We create that experience."

Whether Woodmeister builds a kitchen, a complete home renovation, or an entirely new luxury residence, it uses a unique inside-out engineering approach. The Woodmeister team works collaboratively with the homeowners, architects and interior designers right from the beginning of a project to ensure that every possible detail is thought through and planned before a single board is cut or nailed.

"We actually start our projects at the end," Goodnow explains. "We look at the big picture first, asking ourselves, 'How do all of the pieces of this project need to fit together when it's finished?' We painstakingly think about every detail first and engineer all potential problems before we begin construction." Goodnow gives as an example a recent high-rise renovation project in which Woodmeister engineered expansion joints in the millwork to allow for building sway. By integrating all systems in the design stage, the final components fit together flawlessly and work seamlessly. This, according to Goodnow, is a crucial part of creating the Woodmeister experience of exclusivity and perfection.

The company's surgical approach to its work makes it especially adept at handling city renovation projects with their complex logistics, involving strict condo association rules, city ordinances and difficult mobilization. "Coordinating a multi-million-dollar renovation project on a 35th floor in downtown Boston requires excruciatingly complicated planning and procedures. Our goal is to make sure that no one but ourselves are inconvenienced," Goodnow states.

Another Woodmeister trademark is a three-prong customer service commitment: a *risk-free* guarantee on all projects, *turn-key* customer-centered project management, and a *worry-free* continuous care program. "We are absolutely committed to making sure that working with Woodmeister is a thoroughly enjoyable experience for our customers — at all stages of the process. We assume every risk and every worry both during the project and afterward," says Goodnow. The success of this approach is evident in the company's post-project surveys. Woodmeister customers often comment that it is the attention to the "little things" that made the real difference for them. According to Goodnow, the company strives for more than complete customer satisfaction. "We want our clients to feel pure delight with both the finished product and the process of getting there."

Earning and maintaining the distinction of being a world-class company from both its customers' and employees' perspectives might seem a daunting job for almost any CEO. Looking to the future, Goodnow says the company will continue to embrace innovation as a *Master Builder*, and through it's strategic partnerships and alliances, will continue to be a leader in the luxury home market. Goodnow continues to exude confidence, excitement and energy about the business he created 25 years ago. "We at Woodmeister are proud of the work we do and service we provide. My wife, Kim, and I are grateful for the trust our clients, friends and employees have placed in us over the years, and we look forward to another 25 years of building strong, long-lasting relationships."

CURRY PRINTING

Curry Printing has seen the printing industry go through major changes over the two decades they've been in business in Central Massachusetts. From traditional typesetting and "mechanical art" that was used to make metal printing plates, to high-resolution electronic files that arrive via high-speed phone lines, Curry has kept pace with the technological advances to provide their customers with the latest printing and copying solutions.

It all started in 1978 when Paul Curry opened a small copy shop on Main Street in Worcester. Three years later, he sold it to brothers Tom and Joe Gardner, who had both previously worked for A.B. Dick Co., a major national supplier of printing and copying equipment, and were looking for a business of their own to buy. Tom will tell you he's not a printer, but simply a businessman who owns a printing company; nevertheless, printing seems to be in the family blood because a third brother, Peter, joined the company two years later. Curry Printing now owns and operates locations in Worcester, Auburn, and Westboro as well as a campus copy center at Clark University.

Today, Curry Printing is no longer the simple copy shop it was when Paul Curry opened for business in 1978. Instead, the company has evolved into an award-winning commercial printer specializing in digital printing. This year, Curry received three top awards at the prestigious PrintImage Excellence Awards in Florida; in 2004, Curry was named one of the Top 100 quick printers in the country. In fact, Curry has steadily improved its ranking over the years, going from 98th in 1992 to 70th in 1996, up to 49th last year.

With state-of-the-art equipment including complete electronic pre-press systems for Macintosh and Windows platforms, on-demand digital printing using the latest Canon and Xerox imaging systems, and traditional offset printing on Heidelberg, A.B. Dick, and Ryobi presses, Curry stands ready to deliver the highest quality commercial printing to customers large and small. Its 24-hour, seven-days-a week on-line Customer Service Center even enables customers to place orders, request estimates and review proofs anytime, anywhere. Recently, Curry added direct mail fulfillment to its long list of products and services, providing customers with everything from on-demand printing of direct mail pieces that can be individually customized, to merging mail lists, zip-sorting for the lowest possible mailing rates, and shipping or mailing the completed pieces.

Because of its comprehensive list of products and services, Curry finds itself in the unique position of being a one-stop printing resource for many corporate customers who look to the company for everything from bread-and-butter business cards, letterhead and envelopes to sophisticated six-color corporate sales pieces and everything in between. Curry has found a lucrative niche providing IT training companies and software developers with support and training documentation, such as man-

ABOVE: CURRY MAINTAINS A FLEET OF DELIVERY VANS TO ENSURE THAT CUSTOMERS RECEIVE THEIR JOBS AS QUICKLY AS POSSIBLE

LEFT: A CURRY PREPRESS TECHNICIAN USES THE LATEST DIGITAL TECHNOLOGY TO GET A JOB READY FOR PRESS

The printer scored 100% in both categories.

It's no fluke that Curry Printing won coveted Kronos Premier Supplier Award. "We've worked very hard at developing and implementing the processes necessary to take a job efficiently and flawlessly from entry to delivery," states Joe Gardner. "Every step of every job is tracked and documented so we know at all times where every job is. As a result of the thoroughness of our processes, we have been awarded ISO9001/2000 certification."

But what sets Curry Printing apart from all the other commercial printers in Central Massachusetts isn't just hardware and software. It's the company's commitment to both customers and employees. Although it may sound clichè, Curry really does foster a family-type atmosphere among its employees — encouraging them to make suggestions, offering bonuses both for individuals and teams; and holding monthly meetings in which employees can voice their concerns, discuss issues and get the latest news from management. As a result, customers rate Curry very high for quality, commitment and helpfulness. "Treating your customers and your employees right does make a difference," notes Tom Gardner.

ABOVE: A COMPUTERIZED TRACKING SYSTEM ENABLES EMPLOYEES TO KNOW WHERE EVERY JOB IS IN THE PRINTING PROCESS BELOW: CURRY'S FOUR-COLOR DIRECT IMAGE PRESS PROVIDES SHARP, ACCURATE, COLORFUL PRINTING NO MATTER HOW LARGE OR SMALL THE JOB

uals, guide books and instructional materials; doing everything from pre-press work and printing right through to fulfillment — including sorting, kitting, packaging and shipping. They've become so adept at it, Curry Printing was named Premier Supplier of the Year by Kronos, a leading international workforce management company headquartered in Chelmsford, Mass. To receive this award, Curry had to meet near-perfect quality and delivery requirements for a minimum of 12 consecutive months.

"It's simple," adds Pete Gardner. "Our mission statement is posted in each of our facilities and it reads: 'Our mission is to exceed client expectations by providing the highest-quality product possible in a timely manner. We create long-lasting, prosperous relationships with our client partners in order to help them reach their goals and objectives.'"

SERVICE NETWORK INC.

ervice Network Inc. continues a long tradition of machine tool manufacture in Central Massachusetts.

The year 1984 was not a good one for Worcester-area machine tool companies. In fact, some of those were forced to announce manpower layoffs or to offer early retirement programs, both of which resulted in making many dozens of skilled and experienced technicians available for new jobs.

Seizing this opportunity, Edward Camp, one of the early retirees, incorporated Service Network Inc. (SNI) on September 1, 1984, with the intention of offering a network of servicemen to industry. The idea worked, and the service business grew steadily and, later, expanded to include high-performance grinding machines, both new and remanufactured.

Starting with a humble $2,000 original capital investment, first-year revenues were $65,000 (an acceptable supplement to a retirement income). As the extent of service and product repairs increased, second-year revenues were $450,000. and third-year sales were $750,000. From that point, SNI's sales increased to nearly $11 million.

About year two, SNI was forced to rent factory space to avoid compromising its customers' own production spaces. As things stand now, SNI has outgrown previous locations in Princeton and Auburn, and now has 30,000 square feet of factory and office space in Worcester.

As SNI has grown, so have its product offerings. A recent tally gives SNI credit for more than 125 new inventions and product developments over the years. Some of these have been relatively small, such as new wheel dressing and/or workpiece loading arrangements. Others are more substantial, including the new proprietary internal grinding machines, the SN200/1000-I series, plus the new OEM external diameter grinders, the SN-200/800-E series. In addition, SNI's new Hi-Rez systems should be mentioned. These systems lift older machines into the 21st century and boost accuracies to 10 millionths of an inch, for a small fraction of the cost of a new machine and/or rebuilding. In effect, SNI's product development efforts are continuous, and enable our global competitiveness. Most of SNI's new products are the result of listening to customers. SNI consistently employs the latest grinding technologies in product offerings.

Much of the product development work involved in our new ID and OD grinding machines, as well as

in the new Hi-Rez systems, occurred in the years 2000 to 2004 — which, in the machine tool industry, marked the most severe recession the capital goods industry had seen for more than 45 years. Many of SNI's former competitors went bankrupt. Without the sales impetus provided by our new products, SNI might have followed suit.

Following the recession, SNI's customer base has remained loyal and has returned with expanded

ABOVE: REVIEWING EQUIPMENT SPECIFICATIONS WITH CLIENTS. HUNDREDS OF CUSTOMERS FROM ALL OVER THE WORLD COME TO SNI'S WORCESTER FACILITY YEARLY

BELOW: PARTIAL VIEW OF MAIN MACHINE ASSEMBLY AREA SHOWING BOTH NEW AND REBUILT MACHINES IN PROGRESS

force SNI's strong reputation and act to the benefit of all concerned. Most of these take time and interactive experience to be perceived as real.

Firstly, there is our personnel. All of SNI's engineers and more than 40% of our total workforce hold college/university degrees. All employees are or have been carefully selected for their skills, knowledge, experience and motivations relative to the role each plays at SNI. Collaboration with academia on student internships is strongly encouraged. Also, we foster hiring and training younger employees so that our average employee age trend becomes lower over time.

Secondly, there is our integrity. Integrity is easy to have when the sun is shining. It's only when problems arise that the true mettle of an organization is exposed. In one case, SNI was surprised to learn that, after five years in their plant, a customer was not pleased with an SNI machine. SNI took it back on an "under warranty" arrangement, examined and modified the machine and returned it to production. The machine is now regarded as "the best machine in the plant."

Thirdly, SNI does what it does best. We design, market, assemble and test internal, external and rotary surface grinding machines. SNI is surrounded by very capable chipmaking shops and we are pleased to pay them several million dollars per year for our component parts requirements.

Fourthly, we make partnerships. With customers, vendors and employees SNI believes in the long-term benefits of working together to achieve mutually rewarding objectives. As with many things it takes time to nurture the bilateral trust, attitudes and mutual respect needed for full recognition of the concept. Nevertheless, it has been SNI's experience that the eventual results are well worth the time and efforts involved.

Service Network Inc. is proud of its part in continuing the machine-tool manufacturing legacy in Central Massachusetts and in building its future.

strength and vigor. Markets include a large majority of the U.S.A. bearing industry, plus automotive applications, aerospace, military installations, tool and die work, and others requiring high metalworking precision.

After more than 20 years in business, SNI has become a global player, having shipped equipment to England, Wales, Ireland, Canada, Mexico, India, Austria, China, Romania, Japan, Israel, Germany, the Netherlands, Turkey, Poland and elsewhere.

The resurgence in new business in the U.S.A. since the recession, plus SNI's additional penetration of foreign customer accounts, is raising new business levels by a factor of three to four times (for the year 2005 over the year 2004).

There are several components to SNI's underlying philosophy, which, over the years, have served to rein-

PHOTO/KATHY SANDSTROM

ALEXANDRIA REAL ESTATE EQUITIES/ MASSACHUSETTS BIOMEDICAL INITIATIVES

lexandria Real Estate Equities Inc. (NYSE:ARE) is the pre-eminent international real estate investment trust focused principally on the ownership, operation, management, acquisition, redevelopment and selective development of properties containing office/laboratory space — a niche which we pioneered.

Alexandria has an outstanding eight-year track record as a NYSE-listed company with an approximate $2.85 billion total market capitalization (as of Dec. 31, 2004). We provide high-quality laboratory facilities (such as the Massachusetts Biomedical Initiatives facility in Worcester), services and capital to the broad and diverse life-science sector.

Our clients include institutional (universities and not-for-profit institutions), pharmaceutical, biotechnology, life science product, service, biodefense and translational medicine entities, as well as government agencies.

Alexandria's national operating platform is based on the principle of "clustering," with assets and operations strategically located in key life-science hub markets. Our life-science real estate industry leadership will ultimately help address significant unmet medical needs.

WORCESTER-BASED LABORATORY SPACE AVAILABLE

WAC CONSULTING

AC Consulting provides and supports accounting, manufacturing/warehousing and CRM software solutions, offers software customization service and designs end-to-end solutions that fit each company individually. With its staff of eight, the company offers more than 100 years of combined technical and business experience with advanced degrees in business, finance, engineering and APICS/CPIM certification. The staff also brings real-world experience in finance and accounting, manufacturing workflow processes, materials management, engineering data management and sales force automation to companies both large and small.

The company was founded in 1987 with a simple goal in mind — to help other companies improve their profitability by streamlining business processes and operations. Originally, the company offered a variety of services, including training, network infrastructure and custom solutions before settling on its current focus of supporting an integrated business solution.

In the late 1980s, WAC Consulting was already working with small to medium-sized businesses well before it was trendy, and now it has built a reputation of quality service for almost 20 years.

In 1994 the company was recognized by *Business Week*, a national magazine, in an article about small-business development and the effect of current trends in technology. In the magazine, Robert Distler, founder and principal, emphasized the need to understand the client's business before suggesting the solution of computerization.

"When small-business people come in and want to automate, the first question I ask is: 'Why?'" says Distler, president of WAC Consulting Inc. which sells financial and manufacturing systems. As a first step, he suggests doing a needs analysis to determine what, if anything, can be gained from putting in automation, according to the article that was published in November, 1994.

Through that exposure and a growing need for companies to leverage technology to stay competitive, WAC Consulting gained clients throughout New England and now provides services to companies from as far away as Texas, North Carolina and California.

With the increasing integration of technology into the workplace, WAC Consulting sees the need for its highly trained staff to help small to medium-sized companies determine how to remain competitive by utilizing technology wisely. The company can help the client identify needed changes along with developing a plan to design and implement them. WAC's staff begins by creating a

needs analysis that documents the current processes, learns how the business is run and where it sees itself in the future. With that knowledge in hand, the staff will develop a new technology plan and assist the client with its implementation.

With technology becoming increasingly complex, the staff is continually updating its skills in business analysis, software development, network infrastructure and security. The key to the company's success in the future is its perpetual growth and reputation for having the most highly qualified consultants on board.

ABOVE: RICK DiMARZIO, PRESIDENT OF KREST PRODUCTS CORP. OF LEOMINSTER, STANDS WITH BOB DISTLER IN FRONT OF THE EQUIPMENT USED IN THE MANUFACTURING OF KREST COMBS BELOW: TRAINING SESSION IN FULL SWING AT WAC CONSULTING

AA TRANSPORTATION CO. INC.

Ron Ernenwein, the owner of AA Transportation, has often heard the comment, "You look like a young guy, how did you get here?" As a teenager, his family had a friend who was a successful real estate investor. Ernenwein became inspired by that friend and aspired to be in that industry. Just after he graduated with his associate's degree from Quinsigamond Community College, Ernenwein immediately started to invest in the multi-family real estate market. Over time, he learned how to buy houses with little capital available by utilizing low-money- or no-money-down mortgage programs.

For a short time following college, Ernenwein also worked for a Ford dealer. He had previously worked for the Weagle Bus Co. as a mechanic — he was a family friend. In 1992, he became a full-time maintenance director for the bus company. Soon after that transition, the Weagle family lost its largest contract, the Shrewsbury Public Schools, to a national provider. The family business had held that contract for 72 years.

Ernenwein decided to stay on with Weagle to try and help the family through what would be a very challenging time. The family company was in a very competitive industry, where the lowest bidder always got the contract. As the company downsized, Ernenwein's responsibilities expanded to include overseeing almost every aspect of daily operations.

In 1996, the Weagle Bus Company was dissolved and Ernenwein was faced with another difficult decision — what to do now? As the owners of the company scurried to assign the school routes that they were contractually bound to fulfill to other companies, Ernenwein began to think that perhaps he should be in business for himself.

All the pieces were falling into place; now Ernenwein just needed financing. He did not have the resources to take over the whole company of about 100 vehicles, nor did all the routes make good financial sense. After reviewing his real estate portfolio, the lending company approved him for financing 26 vehicles and he was in business. He began with just a few clients, like the Webster School Department and Assabet Valley Regional Vocational High School.

Business was good and sales doubled year after year. It seemed like every year he added another major customer — like the town of Sutton, then the Lexington Metco Program, followed by Holy Name High School, Abby Kelley Foster Regional Charter School and Assabet Valley Collaborative.

In March 2005, AA Transportation was awarded the contract to transport students of the Shrewsbury

Public schools, adding 50 vehicles and 60 employees to the company, beginning in September, 2005. This was the very contract that the Weagles lost in 1992. Also in 2005, the company added the Southbridge Public Schools to its client list.

At one point, while trying to improve the effi-

Above: Ron Ernenwein

President/CEO

Left: AA Transportation

transports approximately

10,000 children to school

every day

ABOVE: AERIAL SHOT OF HOME OFFICE

BELOW: THE INNOVATIVE 41-PASSENGER LIMO BUS

ciency of the infrastructure and existing overhead, Ernenwein thought of adding a limousine division. He brought the West Coast trend of Hummer and SUV limousines to the Worcester area; this put the company on the cutting edge. To date that division has grown to total more than 10% of their sales. In 2005, the company celebrated nine years and Ernenwein now has 225 vehicles and 300 employees.

Another question often posed to Ernenwein is "What is your secret to success?"

Along with a whole lot of luck, Ernenwein lives by the philosophy of three key factors.

First, he makes himself available for every customer who has a problem. He says an absentee management team does not work, nor can you run a company from the golf course, so he stays involved in overseeing the daily operations personally.

Second, he treats every employee with respect and appreciation. He says that he never forgets one thing, "To provide good quality service, you need good quality, happy employees," he says. "It's not rocket science."

And third, he also has acts on every opportunity. "If you never get up at bat, you can never hit a home run," he says. "I try to look at every opportunity and try to find a way to make it work."

PENTA COMMUNICATIONS INC.

ENTA Communications Inc. is a leading regional marketing firm headquartered in Central Massachusetts. The firm maintains a strong commitment to helping its client companies grow, its employees thrive and its community prosper. For nearly 20 years, the firm has maintained a reputation of excellence for its creativity and its commitment to the community.

Located in the heart of the Corridor Nine area in Westboro, PENTA Communications Inc. has provided marketing, advertising and public relations services to companies throughout New England. Founded in 1988 by entrepreneur Deborah Penta, the firm is recognized throughout the region for its world-class marketing services. PENTA has helped clients in virtually every industry, from consumer-direct to business-to-business. With a goal of strengthening client brand awareness and achieving greater results from clients' marketing and advertising programs, the firm continues to retain existing clients and welcome new companies to its family.

Today, the firm has clients throughout the New England region and the Eastern seaboard. Among its diverse service offerings, PENTA practice areas include strategic marketing, design, advertising campaigns, media planning and buying, direct marketing programs, public relations, Web site design and development, search engine optimization strategies and customer/client retention programs.

Realistically evaluating a client's goals and offering sound advise, answers and solutions are pivotal for success. It is that premise on which PENTA Communications Inc. bases its business.

Continuous improvement and willingness to change is challenging for any company. PENTA Communications strives to be the best in quality of service, results achieved for clients, reputation and client satisfaction. It is this ongoing mission that drives technological enhancements, continuous internal analyses of strengths and weaknesses, and the quest to improve. Clients benefit from PENTA's management-driven passion for each Associate to raise the bar in all facets of its services to satisfy its clients.

Staying abreast of trends and technologies is a key component of the organization's strategy. Understanding that each client has its own unique needs is of the utmost importance at the firm. There are no "cookie-cutter" marketing answers at PENTA Communications Inc. Each marketing plan is tailor-made to fit the client's requirements.

Clients benefit from their association with PENTA through measurable changes such as increasing visibility, enhancing image and inspiring customer confidence.

PENTA Communications Inc. has a variety of market surveys and customer feedback analyses to show each company its overall strengths and weaknesses, which will assist in finding missed opportunities.

PENTA Communications Inc. has a strong social commitment to its community and has helped many non-profit organizations throughout the state of Massachusetts, gearing its mission to helping children. The company, along with the assistance of many of its clients, has raised nearly a half-million dollars to benefit children's charities since its inception.

In addition, the company encourages active participation with schools and engages in mentoring programs, internship hosting and proudly sponsors the Deborah A. Penta Female Leadership Scholarship, awarded annually to college-bound high school women who have demonstrated exemplary leadership ability.

ABOVE: WITH OFFICES IN WORCESTER AND BOSTON, PENTA COMMINICATIONS INC. MEETS THE NEEDS OF ITS CLIENTS
BELOW: DEBORAH A. PENTA, CEO PENTA COMMUNICATIONS INC.

BEECHWOOD HOTEL

*S*et in the heart of Central Massachusetts, the Beechwood Hotel offers the best of all possible worlds.

This luxury, boutique property is located in a quiet park-like setting, yet is only minutes from downtown Worcester and the excitement of major music, entertainment and sports venues.

The Beechwood Hotel's elegant architecture and sophisticated dècor make an immediate impact, from its unique circular structure, lush landscaped grounds and outdoor patio, to its gracious foyer with its magnificent stained-glass ceiling.

Over the years, the Beechwood Hotel has been the preferred destination for those who expect nothing less than the best while visiting the Greater Worcester area. Only the Beechwood Hotel provides the world-class accommodations, dining and ambience of a big city hotel, together with the relaxed, informal attitude and warm, personal attention of a classic New England inn. The result is a unique blend of amenities and services unmatched anywhere in the region.

The beautifully appointed and newly renovated guest rooms each have their own charming personality and many offer cathedral ceilings, skylights and fireplaces. The hotel's Grand Ballroom is simply breathtaking, with elegant cathedral ceilings and handsome maple wood trim creating a spacious but inviting atmosphere, which is heightened by the adjoining 100-year-old Maria Gill Wilson Room, a reconstructed and fully restored classic Victorian-style chapel. The chapel was formerly located at the Worcester City Hospital, and was meticulously disassembled and reconstructed in its present site.

All of the hotel's 73 guest rooms and suites offer a complementary continental breakfast, complementary phone calls within the United States, high-speed Internet connection, an iron and ironing board, a hair dryer and plush robes. The facility offers 24-hour room service, fitness center, business center, gift shop and complementary parking.

At the Beechwood Hotel, you'll find they not only meet their guests' needs, they anticipate them. It's their unflagging commitment to exceptional service that is both friendly and genuine. This philosophy turns guests at the hotel into friends of the hotel. And those friends return to the hotel year after year. Many famous guests have also stayed at the hotel while visiting the area.

The Beechwood Hotel's award-winning restaurant offers classic and New American-style cuisine that delights both the eye and the palate. It has been the area's unanimous choice for fine dining. The

restaurant was recently voted a "Best of Worcester" destination by *Worcester Magazine*, and awarded an exceptionally rare 5-star rating. Guests can select from an impressive array of classic and New American dishes, from fresh native seafood to prime beef, to handmade pastas, fresh sauces and delicate desserts. All meals are expertly prepared and presented by our award-winning executive chef and staff.

Sunday brunch is also offered at the restaurant, which is a favorite of many area residents each week since the restaurant is open to the public.

Recent multi-million-dollar renovations have further enhanced the charm and comfort of a stay at the Beechwood. An example of these improvements is the Grand Ballroom. With seating for up to 350 guests, the magnificent room is the perfect setting for social and business meetings as well as weddings. The hotel also renovated all rooms and suites, as well as adding a luxurious Presidential Suite.

Indeed, this luxury hotel provides guests with the best of all possible worlds.

ABOVE: THE BEECHWOOD HOTEL IS A LUXURY, BOUTIQUE HOTEL WITH A UNIQUE BLEND OF AMENITIES AND SERVICES BELOW: GUESTS MAY RELAX IN THE WARM, STYLISH FIRE-LIT LOBBY

BOLLUS LYNCH

ollus Lynch Certified Public Accountants and Consultants knows the value of combining national-level accounting experience and resources with local, personalized service and an individualized business perspective. Each of our five partners brings more than a decade of national accounting-firm experience to our Worcester-based practice. In fact, our firm's partners have combined national and local experience that exceeds 100 years.

Perhaps that's why so many of our clients, nearly 80%, are former customers of national CPA firms. From manufacturers to contractors to museums and colleges, the diverse array of businesses that count on Bollus Lynch for audit, tax and general business advisory services have discovered that our quality, style and philosophy not only measure up to those of our big-firm counterparts, but often surpass them.

Taking a page from the philosophy of national firms, we offer specialized industry practices to such clients as manufacturers, construction firms, not-for-profits and financial institutions. In keeping with our local focus and commitment to serve Central Mass. companies in the $1-million to $200-million range, however, we strive to be as practical and cost-effective as possible. And we stay on top of the changing marketplace and regulatory climate to ensure our clients get continuous first-rate service.

When a company becomes a client of Bollus Lynch, they don't just become a client of one of our partners. Each of our customers is served by our entire firm, with all the resources and expertise that we collectively have to offer.

Unlike some smaller CPA firms that only gear up for tax time, Bollus Lynch remains a stable financial resource for your firm throughout the year. We not only offer expertise on financial statements, audits and tax preparation, we also assist companies with their budget and forecast needs, all-important internal audit services, merger and acquisition consultation, estate tax planning, business evaluations, on-site accounting training and even litigation support, should the need arise. Should your company need the resources of a national-level firm, Bollus Lynch is a member of

an alliance with one of the largest national accounting and consulting firms in the country, BDO Seidman LLP.

Serving the Central Massachusetts region since 1989, Bollus Lynch's main office is ideally located in downtown Worcester and is fully automated with state-of-the-art technology. Our accounting, auditing and tax library and its publication services is the most advanced and complete of any firm our size in this region.

ALLEGRO MICROSYSTEMS INC.

Allegro MicroSystems Inc. is a global leader in the development, manufacture and marketing of advanced semiconductor products, including Hall-effect sensors and analog power integrated circuits. Allegro MicroSystems is the successor to the Sprague Semiconductor Group, which established the Worcester site in 1965 as a manufacturing facility. Today, the Worcester site, employing 800 people, is Allegro's headquarters. Worldwide, Allegro, with sales of $280 million, employs 2,400 associates in facilities in North America, Europe and Asia.

Our innovative, system-level solutions serve high-growth applications within the automotive, computer/office automation, industrial, consumer and communications markets, while our leading-edge product and processes reinforce our expertise in motor driver and power management technology. We are a world leader in automotive sensing electronics and integrated Hall-effect magnetic sensors. Within the automotive area, our products serve electronic applications within virtually all automotive brands. In fact, more than 200 million Allegro devices are installed in automotive applications each year. In addition, we also hold leading positions within printer, scanner, copier and portable device (e.g. cellular phones) applications.

With global manufacturing capabilities and more than 200 patents, our product development expertise is supported by our strong knowledge of electronic systems and unique capabilities in the areas of silicon wafer processing and integrated circuit package development. These skills enable us to deliver application-specific, system-level solutions for virtually all power and sensing applications within our chosen markets. Our world-class expertise and reputation for quality have also enabled us to develop long-term relationships with leading customers in each market segment. Our team of design and systems engineers is uniquely capable of translating customer needs to innovative solutions and is focused on continuously reducing design time and cost.

Our global manufacturing sources provide world-class quality, delivery and cost performance. Allegro is recognized for its quality systems and has received quality awards from leading manufacturers worldwide, IECQ manufacturers' approval, QS 9000 and ISO 9001 registration.

Within the Worcester community, Allegro actively supports organizations and foundations with a

special focus on activities that support education, health, the environment and children. Our corporate efforts are supported by those of our associates and their families, who generously donate their time and talent to a variety of local activities.

Allegro recognizes that its success has been built on the dedication, commitment and talent of its associates. Our business growth and profitability have enabled ongoing investment in facilities, equipment and people. We will remain a worldwide leading supplier of analog integrated products through our focused efforts to provide value to customers, offer technically advanced products, continuously improve in all areas of our organization and maintain a positive work environment for our associates.

ABOVE: A VIEW OF ALLEGRO'S HIGH-TEMPERATURE OVENS FOR DIFFUSING PROCESS CHEMICALS INTO THE SURFACE OF SILICON WAFERS

BELOW: ALLEGRO MICROSYSTEMS' CORPORATE HEADQUARTERS ON 115 NORTHEAST CUTOFF IN WORCESTER

WORCESTER PUBLISHING LTD.

ince 1990, Worcester Publishing Ltd. has been delivering award-winning reportage and analysis to readers throughout Central Massachusetts. From boardroom issues to neighborhood concerns to cultural commentary, its business and consumer publications have established strong reader and advertiser followings in their respective niches. Its specialty publishing division has designed and produced the book you hold in your hands right now.

Worcester Publishing Ltd. was founded 15 years ago by Chairman Allen Fletcher, who, along with Publisher Peter Stanton, were determined to pursue their publishing goals despite a regional recession. The company's first titles, appearing in the spring of 1990, were the *Worcester Business Journal* — a biweekly business-to-business publication — and Inside Worcester, a glossy city magazine. While the magazine eventually fell victim to the continuing recession, the *Worcester Business Journal* flourished and has established itself as the most highly regarded source of business news and information in Central Massachusetts and the MetroWest region.

The *Journal* is recognized as an agenda-setter on a variety of municipal and regional issues, particularly urban development, where its voice has filled a significant void in the region. The paper has garnered numerous editorial, advertising and design awards,

including a national first prize for General Excellence given by the Association of Area Business Publications. Annual issues such as the *Book of Lists* and *Fact Book* have become indispensable to local business readers, along with special feature sections within its regular, bi-weekly publishing cycle.

Seeking to capitalize on its proven success with the *Worcester Business Journal*, the company founded a sister publication in Hartford, Connecticut, in 1992 — the *Hartford Business Journal*. This publication has established its own niche and strong following in that capital city. In 1996, the publication increased its frequency from biweekly to weekly, helping to solidify its current strong presence in the Hartford region.

The company also expanded on its business to business franchise in December, 1992, when it purchased *Worcester Magazine*, injecting new life into

five times — including 2003, 2004 and 2005.

The company added at third business publication to its portfolio in 1999, when it purchased the young monthly journal, *MaineBiz*, in Portland, Maine. Now bi-weekly, it has established itself as the leading business-to-business magazine in the state. It has captured numerous national design and editorial awards, including first place for General Excellence in both 2004 and 2005.

From an original staff of 17, Worcester Publishing has grown to employ a talented staff of more than 70 individuals in its Worcester, Hartford and Portland offices. In doing so, it continues to fulfill several of its key missions — to provide editorial value to its readers, commercial value to its advertisers and social value for everyone within its organization. Located on Shrewsbury Street, the Worcester office has helped to anchor the continuing rebirth of that East Side commercial thoroughfare, and sits at the gateway to the city's downtown renaissance.

In harmony with a company ethic of civic involvement, Worcester Publishing Ltd. provides sponsorships and donations to dozens of charitable and cultural endeavors. Its employees participate enthusiastically in local nonprofit organizations, cultural and civic groups and business associations.

ABOVE: (L-R) CHIEF OPERATING OFFICER PETER STANTON, CHAIRMAN ALLEN FLETCHER AND CHIEF FINANCIAL OFFICER CRAIG THORNTON

BELOW: (L-R) WORCESTER BUSINESS JOURNAL MANAGING EDITOR CHRISTINA O'NEILL, WORCESTER MAGAZINE PUBLISHER DIANE LIEBERMAN, WORCESTER BUSINESS JOURNAL ASSOCIATE PUBLISHER MARK MURRAY, INFORMATION TECHNOLOGY DIRECTOR PETER WILSON, WORCESTER MAGAZINE EDITOR MICHAEL WARSHAW AND WORCESTER BUSINESS JOURNAL DIRECTOR OF MARKETING AND DEVELOPMENT BONNIE LEROUX

the weekly, general-interest publication. The publication is currently undergoing another facelift scheduled for a fall, 2005 launch, as it heads into its 30th year of publication. Its progress has paralleled the growth and development of the city it serves, reaching new levels of editorial and advertising excellence. The paper exercises a highly respected editorial voice, and serves as an indispensable source of news, arts and entertainment information for the region. *Worcester Magazine* has earned its share of prestigious awards for content and design over the years, including being named Newspaper of the Year by the New England Press Association an impressive

CHARTER COMMUNICATIONS

C harter Communications came to Worcester in July, 1999, when it purchased Greater Media. Since 1999, Charter has employed more than 500 people in Central and Western Massachusetts.

Charter Communications began in cable television more than a decade ago. In 1993, the small company was founded to provide analog video to homes. Now Charter makes access to all the latest communication and entertainment technology affordable, useful and fun.

Today, Charter Communications is a Fortune 500 company that provides the cutting-edge in digital entertainment and communications for the home.

When Charter was founded, Charter Communications Chairman Paul Allen envisioned a wired world — a global broadband network that would interconnect every home that would include television, computers, the Internet and communications.

Now Charter offers a full range of advanced broadband services to the home, including cable television on an advance digital video-programming platform via Charter Digital and Charter High Speed Internet Service. They also provide business-to-business video, data and Internet protocol solutions through the Charter Business division.

The companies provides digital cable, high-speed Internet, HDTV, pay-per-view/video on demand, DVR (digital video recorder), and the newest product — Charter Telephone — to customers in Central and Western Massachusetts and these products are available to Charter customers today.

With the ability to transmit voice, video and data at high speed, cable is the primary platform for delivering these services to the home and workplace. The vision of the company is to become the leader in providing in-home technology.

Since the company began in the mid-1990s, Charter has been committed to providing high-quality customer service, the latest technology and a wide variety of video programming at an affordable price. As the company has grown globally, their commitment to the customer has grown as well.

In the future, Charter hopes to bring wired-world

accessibility to as many people as possible. With new technologies available every day, Charter is realizing new efficiencies from a more uniform approach to service, pricing, customer procedures and operations.

Though a company operating across the world, Charter Communications has a philosophy that stresses the importance of local management making local decisions that affect customers.

With more than 15,500 employees nationwide in more than 4,200 locations, Charter is committed to quickly respond to broadband communications needs, wherever they may be.

Charter also provides support to local communities through civic and charitable organizations. More than 9,000 schools benefit from Charter's Cable in the Classroom program, which provides free cable connections and programming along with high-speed data in schools.

WORCESTER REGIONAL TRANSIT AUTHORITY

The Worcester Regional Transit Authority (WRTA) is a crucial economic link for the city of Worcester and its surrounding communities. The service provided by the WRTA fills an essential mobility need for commuters, the elderly, the mobility impaired, low-income families, college students and environmentally minded citizens. The WRTA provides access to healthcare facilities, grocery stores, shopping centers, jobs and tourist attractions. It is a safe, inexpensive way for citizens to be contributing members of our regional economy.

The WRTA has been providing service since 1974. During that time the WRTA has worked continuously to improve its efficiency while coping with and tightly managing state reductions. The WRTA is a public agency created by the state Legislature.

"Our desire is to strategically allocate our limited resources so that we reach the maximum number of people. A reliable and responsive transportation system is also imperative to the economic growth in the region. We hope to be a vital resource to planners and developers and others who are working hard to position Worcester as both a hub of tourism and business in New England," says WRTA Administrator Mary L. MacInnes.

As a result of a service-wide study, an action plan was developed and approved in 2005 that will provide the most productive service and assist the greatest number of people. The five-year plan calls for increasing service to important locations such as Union Station for MBTA commuter rail connections and to the UMass Memorial Medical Center. Phase I will be implemented in January, 2006, with each successive phase rolling out 6-9 months thereafter.

"The skyline of downtown Worcester will be changing dramatically over the next few years and we are planning for those changes in our system now. Union Station will become a secondary hub for our system and we will increase service in the coming years. We've seen tremendous growth in the outlying communities as people search for affordable housing outside of the Boston area, and we will continuously monitor their needs for public transportation," says MacInnes.

LEFT: ADDITIONAL ROUTES WILL BE STOPPING AT THE UNION STATION INTERMODEL CENTER WHEN THE NEW CHANGES TO THE WRTA SCHEDULE TAKE EFFECT IN JANUARY, 2006
BELOW: THE WRTA OPERATES IN THE CITY OF WORCESTER AND 13 SURROUNDING COMMUNITIES WITH FIXED-ROUTE SERVICE

The WRTA has 43 buses in its fleet and 101 vans and 20-passenger minibuses, and 27 fixed-service routes. It makes an average of 92,453 passenger trips weekly. The WRTA serves 13 surrounding communities, including Auburn, Boylston, Brookfield, Clinton, East Brookfield, Holden, Leicester, Millbury, Oxford, Shrewsbury, Spencer, Webster and West Boylston. The WRTA also provides a variety of special services for elderly and disabled residents in its entire 37-community service area.

PHOTOS/JOHN FERRARONE

UMASS MEMORIAL MEDICAL CENTER

U Mass Memorial Medical Center is the flagship academic medical center of UMass Memorial Health Care, the largest not-for-profit health-care system in Central Massachusetts. In addition to the medical center, the system includes four community hospitals, outpatient services, community-based physician offices, a long-term care facility, and home health, hospice, rehabilitation and mental health services. UMass Memorial is the clinical partner of the University of Massachusetts Medical School.

Our Medical Center is a 725-bed acute care hospital located on three campuses in Worcester: the Memorial Campus, University Campus and Hahnemann Campus. UMass Memorial offers highly sophisticated technology and support services necessary to provide the region with specialists nationally acclaimed for their work in areas such as cardiology, orthopedics, newborn intensive care, hematology/oncology, organ transplantation, children's services, women's services and emergency medicine. The Medical Center is also home to the region's only Trauma Center, supported by LifeFlight, New England's first air ambulance service.

Most high-achieving health-care organizations are known for their centers of excellence that respond to important health-care needs in the community with exceptional programs of care and research. While UMass Memorial continues to provide superior care across the entire spectrum of services, it has achieved recognition for specific programs of care. The UMass Memorial Centers of Excellence are defined by leading-edge care, robust clinical service and advanced training programs.

Our Center of Excellence in Cancer Care provides world-class services to patients in Central Massachusetts and throughout New England. It includes our breast cancer screening program for high-risk patients and intensity modulated radiation therapy, which is one of the most significant treatment breakthroughs in decades. Our Medical Center is also the site of the New England Hemophilia Center. Additionally, UMass Memorial is a regional leader in treating gastrointestinal cancer. The center conducts extensive research and clinical trials, and utilizes the latest discoveries from laboratories and research centers worldwide. Access to these resources enables our specialists to offer the most advanced diagnoses and

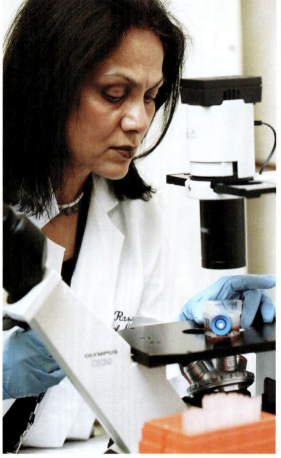

treatments available.

Our Heart and Vascular Center of Excellence offers a full range of integrated patient-care services, including cardiac catheterization, electrophysiology and pacing services, surgical procedures and cardiac rehabilitation. Our Cardiac Catheterization Center features the most advanced technology in the nation for diagnosing and treating heart disease. Our Heart Failure Wellness Center helps those with congestive heart failure live comfortable and

LEFT: KEEPING PACE WITH THE LATEST ADVANCEMENTS IN RESEARCH, AZRA RAZA, MD, CHIEF, DIVISION OF HEMATOLOGY/ONCOLOGY, LEADS SEVERAL CLINICAL TRIALS AND STUDIES TO COMBAT CANCER

BELOW: MARY LEE, MD, CHIEF, PEDIATRIC ENDOCRINOLOGY AND DIABETES PROGRAM, EASES THE FEAR OF YOUNG PATIENTS SEEN IN THE DIABETES CLINIC

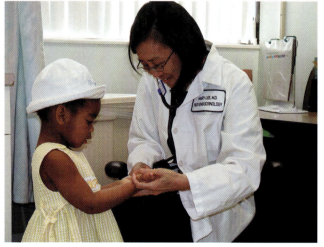

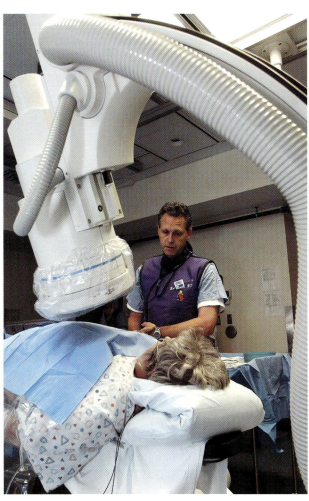

productive lives. Advances in cardiac surgery include minimally invasive mitral valve repair, and ventricular restructuring to re-establish normal size and shape of the heart after being affected by a heart attack. As an academic medical center, our physicians are also researchers. Through ongoing research studies for heart disease, we are making more life-changing discoveries that are available to patients.

Our multidisciplinary team from the Musculoskeletal Center of Excellence care for people with bone, muscle or joint conditions. In the Arthritis and Joint Replacement Center, a team of orthopedic surgeons and rheumatologists offer relief to patients with arthritis and joint disorders. Foot and Ankle Center physicians provide expert care for acute and chronic foot and ankle injuries. Our state-of-the-art Spine Center offers comprehensive care for congenital, degenerative and traumatic spinal disorders in adults and children. The Sports Medicine Center team evaluates and treats all types of sports injuries, from the elite professional athlete to the recreational sports enthusiast. We also offer specialty care programs in hand and upper extremities, pediatrics and orthopedic trauma.

For 25 years, our Central Massachusetts community has turned to UMass Memorial for the region's most advanced emergency and trauma services. Today, our University Campus Emergency Department treats 75,000 patients each year. And because the number continues to grow, UMass Memorial recently opened a 264,000-square-foot, three-story building addition that tripled its Emergency Department space, added new operating suites and intensive care beds, and updated its diagnostic imaging technology. In addition, the new Emergency Department is home to the region's only Level I Trauma Center, and offers emergency mental health services and separate pediatric treatment areas for our younger patients.

In recent years UMass Memorial Medical Center has also introduced a Weight Center, invested in new advanced radiology equipment, opened a comprehensive Women's Center, and expanded Children's Medical Center services.

In addition to the advances in technology and patient care happening every day at our medical center and member hospitals, UMass Memorial has launched many initiatives to promote the health and well-being of Central Massachusetts residents. We partner with the Worcester Housing Authority to provide medical services at public housing sites, support the health-care needs of the uninsured and underinsured. UMass Memorial raised hundreds of thousands of dollars for the American Heart Association through the Worcester Heart Walk, becoming one of the Top 10 donor organizations. In 2005, we announced the UMass Memorial Bell Hill-East Side Homeownership Initiative, a collaboration with city and state agencies to help retain and recruit employees while improving the neighborhoods of Worcester.

As we continue to grow, UMass Memorial Health Care will continue its mission of improving the health of the people of Central Massachusetts. Our academic medical center and member hospitals will continue to achieve patient-focused excellence through the highest standards of quality care, patient safety and patient satisfaction. Our primary care doctors, located in communities throughout Central Massachusetts, will offer adults and children comprehensive and patient-centered care. And through our programs and services we will continue to support the community we serve. Patients in Central Massachusetts will continue to receive access to the highest quality health care available today — all right here in Worcester.

INDEX

ALLEN FLETCHER